WHAT PHILOSOPHY IS

*the text of this book is printed
on 100% recycled paper*

HARPER ESSAYS IN PHILOSOPHY

Edited by Arthur C. Danto

WHAT PHILOSOPHY IS

A GUIDE TO THE ELEMENTS

≫ Arthur C. Danto ≪

HARPER TORCHBOOKS ❡
Harper & Row, Publishers
New York and Evanston

To my Daughter
Jane

WHAT PHILOSOPHY IS

First HARPER TORCHBOOK edition published 1971

STANDARD BOOK NUMBER: 06-131546-X

Contents

III ≪ KNOWLEDGE

IV ≪ THE WORLD

Preface to the Torchbook Edition

> *Now philosophy must discover*
> *the ground of all experience;*
> *thus its object necessarily lies*
> *outside all experience.*
> FICHTE, *The Science of Knowledge.*

A MYTH is an image in terms of which one sees one's life. In a philosophical image, which at times has been a myth, Plato likens the human condition to imprisonment in a cave. That the world is a prison and our life and hope respectively are servitude and release, is a universal image, powerful enough to be transformed into a myth, and hence, to become imprisoning in its own right if it is nonsense or is false. For we then will be held captive only by the belief in our captivity.

Plato's version is the reverse of this, and it is philosophical because it is grounded in the concept of cognition. According to him, our imprisonment consists exclusively of the fact that we are *not* aware of being in our prison. So we cannot (logically) both be in this condition and know that we are in it, and knowledge of our condition is instantly delivering, like a cure for a disease which consists only in not having the cure. But deliverance is complicated by the extraordinary difficulty of explaining to the prisoners, in terms intelligible to them, that prisoners are what they are. For the conditions which make self-understanding possible are incompatible with the conditions they are in, and he who speaks of imprisonment to prisoners must be regarded by them as a madman in his raving. For the bonds which hold them captive are the boundaries of understanding, and how are we to bring the boundaries *within* themselves to make them understood? The limits of understanding are not part of what is understood.

The sum of what the prisoners know is shadows and images of things, projected onto the cave's wall. These compose reality for them. The shadows are the touchstone of intelligibility for creatures in their circumstances, for since shadows are all they know, no statement except one about shadows will be meaningful to them. It is this which makes it difficult, which perhaps makes it impossible, that they should know the limits of their world or even that their world has limits, for how is the expression "only shadows" to be made intelligible in terms which refer alone to shadows? This is a statement made about reality from without, and one who understands reality only from within cannot then know that he does so. Since we cannot have it explained to us, release must be a kind of logical miracle, and, thus, Plato resorted to poetry and image since *literal* explanation was foreclosed.

Of course, an image of a cave might always be projected onto the wall, and even one with images of men within it. What could not be projected onto the wall is the crucial fact that it is a projection, a shadow of the real relationship, for the relationship between shadow and substance is just what cannot be put into the language of shadows. And how, since the men cannot see themselves but only their shadows, are they to know their shadows to be shadows, and to be of *them?* So the deep, redemptive message becomes corrupted and falsified, and unless poetry turns the men round, we cannot really communicate to them even the problems of communication. They must see themselves and their world in a relation which could not be understood in terms of relations within the world as they know it. For that is a world in which shadows are related only to shadows, and the concept of an outside makes no sense. "The understanding," wrote John Locke, "like the eye, whilst it makes us see and perceive all other things, takes no notice of itself; and it requires art and pains to set it at a distance and make it its own object." But what, after all, will *tell* me even then that what I see is what I see with? How shall I understand what makes understanding possible?

Plato, as it happens, was a visionary as well as a philosopher, and the idiom he employed, of shadow and image and appearance, implied the existence of a reality higher and less derivative, which he both believed in and believed that we, too, might behold once led out of the cavern of this world into a higher one of light and goodness. But the problem of understanding, of making understanding understood, is not resolved by postulating another realm of entities, for the very same question must arise with these. To postulate Forms, as Plato did, is an activity of the intellect of a piece with postulating electrons or gods or genes or subconscious, libidinally charged complexes. It is of a piece with science, whose task it is to explain the way the world is and to say what it is made of. It would be an interesting, even an astonishing fact were the world to hold, in addition to the objects of common experience and science, special entities of the sort we associate with Plato's teaching, but it is not a fact of any special philosophical interest if philosophy's concern is with reality from without, with the conditions of intelligibility rather than what is intelligible, with the conditions rather than the content of knowledge. If there were Platonic entities, they would fall on the other side of a line it is the main role of philosophy to bring to consciousness. So philosophy does not contribute especially to our knowledge of reality, nor shall we know, having entered philosophy, anything about reality further than we knew before, except perhaps that it is reality. Nor can we, on the other hand, explain the nature of philosophy in terms which originally and properly pertain to reality, except metaphorically or mythically, as Plato intuitively, if sometimes misleading, appreciated.

The space of philosophy is not a space we enter easily or spontaneously, and because almost everything we understand lies within the world philosophy represents from without, we are at a loss to describe the space of philosophy. And it is easy to misunderstand what philosophy must try to do. The great Danish wit, Kierkegaard, said this:

What the philosophers say about reality is often as disappointing as a sign you see in a shop window, which reads: Pressing Done Here. If you brought your clothes to be pressed, you would be fooled, for the sign is only for sale.

This is a wry joke and a deep one, and only the disappointment is disappointing, for it shows that even Kierkegaard demanded of philosophers that they should talk like scientists or theologians about reality, rather than about—what is their subject—talking about reality.

Philosophy, then, is an attempt to put reality at a certain kind of distance, not so much to see it from without as to get a glimpse of what seeing reality itself consists in. For that reason it is all the more difficult to put philosophy itself at a distance. This perhaps explains why philosophy books seem always to have to say what philosophy itself is, as though their relation to their subject were the subject they were related to. And perhaps it justifies this book, which tries the trick of putting philosophy at a distance by immediately putting the reader inside philosophy.

New York   ARTHUR C. DANTO

Preface

Only where there is language, is there world.
MARTIN HEIDEGGER,
Holdelin and the Essence of Poetry

IN ONE OF HIS logical fantasies, Lewis Carroll describes the bafflement felt by some persons who, in comparing the map of a region with the region itself, discover that the region contains many things which the map does not show. Accordingly, they propose to make the map more "adequate," putting in more and more. Since, however, there remain things in the region which are not duplicated in the map, they conclude that the only adequate map of the region must be the region itself. As do most of Carroll's absurdities, this one has a philosophical thrust. It teaches us something about representation. If the region itself can be its only adequate map, the region will unhappily fail to serve the normal purposes of maps. If, thus, we are *lost* in the region, a map will hardly help to orient us, in case the map turns out to be an exact replica of the region itself, tree for tree, house for house. We realize that a map can only fulfill its primary functions of guidance and location if it is *different* from the territory it represents, and that leaving things out, far from being a blemish or defect in a map, is absolutely requisite if it is to be a map at all. It is, thus, not a criticism of a map that New York, for example, does not really look like a dot.

Acknowledging the logical force of Lewis Carroll's philosophical parable, we must turn our back upon it when we undertake to chart the territory of philosophy. For, as one must quickly come to realize, the only adequate guide to philosophy is philosophy itself. Until one has found one's way about in philosophy, indeed, one hardly is even in a position to understand a *guide* to philosophy. So guides to philosophy seem curiously useless. When one needs them most, they are not understandable; and when they are under-standable, they are not needed at all. A guide to philosophy, unless it is understood *philosophically*, is not *rightly* understood. But how, then, are we to understand a guide philosophically if we do not first know what philosophy is? And how are we to find *that* out without a guide? This state of affairs seems hopeless for those who wish to learn philosophy, and for those who wish to teach it. Yet somehow philosophy is taught and learnt.

Consider the somewhat helpful analogy of learning how to read. In one obvious respect, we cannot learn to read by means of the self-defeating volume entitled "Teach Yourself to Read." We can-not because, if we are to be in a position to *use* the volume, we already know what it has to teach us; and if we do not know this, we cannot read the book at all to benefit from its instructions. So such books are either useless or pointless, as the case may be. Yet reading is taught and learnt. People learn to read by *reading*. There is no other way. Prior to learning what it is to read, a preliterate person may know a *great deal* of the external facts regarding read-ing. He will be able physically to identify books, and perhaps even alphabetical shapes; and he will be able correctly to apply the description "is reading" to persons who are reading. But until he learns to read he cannot really be said to understand what "reading" means or what reading *is*. Nor is there anything in his preliterate experience which can be appealed to as a hopeful *analogy*, so that he at least can be taught what it is *like* to read. No, the only way even to learn what it is like to read is to learn to read. Learning to read *is reading*, albeit haltingly and tentatively.

In learning philosophy, the mere skill of being able to read, while obviously presupposed, can easily mislead the aspirant. For books, after all, look much alike, and anyone who can read the language with fluency can read indifferently well any book in the language, philosophy books included. So it might not occur to him that there are ways and ways of reading books, including quite nonphilosophical ways of reading philosophy books. Many books, for example, are read in order to find out something, and there are certainly books we can read which will tell us about philosophy, just as others can tell us about Africa or trout fishing or marriages.

But one can find out a lot about philosophy—one can know its history and the names of its great masters and even their characteristic, famous doctrines—and not really know what philosophy is. As with reading, one's knowledge will be the external knowledge of the preliterate. One only learns what philosophy is by doing philosophy, by reading *philosophically*. There is no other way. The only way into philosophy is by means of philosophy itself.

No book then can lead its readers into philosophy unless it is a book *in*, and not merely a book about philosophy. This book, thus, is an exploration of the territory to which it simultaneously attempts to be a guide: a contribution as well as a key. And so it is addressed to fellow philosophers as much as to initiates. It begins and ends with the question posed implicitly in this preface: what is philosophy? I have chosen this as my terminal query for it is at once a question about philosophy, and an internal question of philosophy, and so a question to which a philosophical and a nonphilosophical answer can be given. The difference between these, and hence between the philosophical and nonphilosophical *senses* of questions may perhaps best be made conspicuous through a question which has both senses. The only satisfactory answer to the philosophical question, What is philosophy?, is a philosophical answer.

I have *not* tried a strategy, which is often thought suitable, of engaging the prephilosophical reader where he is already apt to be most engaged, namely with questions regarding morality. There is, indeed, very little on this topic in my book, and I will explain its omission now. We are all of us ready to dispute moral questions with passion and conviction and concern. Because there is, in the popular mind, an identification of philosophy with moral inquiry, we are apt to sustain the illusion, when discussing moral issues, that we are engaged in philosophy automatically. But this will almost always be an illusion. And nothing more fatally bars one's entry into philosophy than the false belief that one has entered philosophy already. When, on the other hand, a prephilosopher encounters the sorts of questions which philosophers interested in the topic of morality themselves discuss, these will almost certainly appear so abstract and remote from matters of immediate moment to human beings, that one must conclude that philosophy has scant relevance to our lives. And this, too, can stunt the curiosity for philosophical knowledge.

I have woven into my fabric certain questions of moral philosophy, but in such a way that they may be seen as part of the entire design. The seemingly abstruse questions of philosophical ethics are seen as crucial only when the bearing of their answers upon the wider conceptual queries of philosophy are revealed. One cannot, really, get serious results on any portion of philosophy without keeping the entirety of philosophy always in mind. The parts are intelligible only in the circumference of the whole. This book has, accordingly, a spiral structure, and one ends at the same point at which one began, but hopefully upon a higher plane. To understand the beginning, one must return to it, after having reached the end.

New York   ARTHUR C. DANTO

Acknowledgements

THIS BOOK BEGAN as an introductory essay for the *Harper Guide to Philosophy*, but it quickly took on a life of its own, and virtually wrote itself. I am grateful to Fred Wieck, who first proposed the *Harper Guide* and but for whom, I believe it safe to say, this book would never have been written. I am grateful as well to my editor, Alfred E. Prettyman, of Harper & Row, for his informed enthusiasm and constructive suggestions. Michael Levin commented upon the entire manuscript, and I am much indebted to his philosophical intelligence and critical energy. Bernard Rollin and John Flynn, whose sensibilities and responses I greatly respect, also read through the manuscript. Professor Elinor West, of Long Island University, not only worked through the arguments, but put them promptly into practice with her classes. I am grateful to her, as to these other friends and former students, for the encouragement of their interest. I must thank the charming editor of the enterprising British journal, *Common Factor*, for permission to reprint, as section 49 of this book, a paper I originally published there as a contribution to a symposium on the topic of freedom and determinism. I must finally express my gratitude to the undergraduate students of Columbia College, whose sharp, athletic intelligences contributed immensely in helping me to formulate the issues I lectured to them on.

I ◄◄ PHILOSOPHY

1. In the present temper of their discipline, philosophers would prefer not to have to talk in a general way about philosophy itself. It is difficult to avoid sounding pretentious or edifying when one does so, and neither of these is to the present taste. But such reluctance has, perhaps, a deeper origin. Practitioners of other disciplines are not required, as part of their competence, to be able to specify the essential, general traits of their subject, or even to be able to say in a general way what sorts of problems they deal with. It may be that the nature, say, of physics, is not a problem *in* physics at all: it is an external question to which one may, while remaining a fine or even a great physicist, have no answer, or simply a bad answer. But then it is not counted a failure in the discipline, or among its practitioners, if one cannot answer external questions about the discipline itself. It is enough that the practitioners of a discipline should be able to answer internal questions, that is, be successful practitioners of their discipline. Poets and musicians, like scientists and historians, must distinguish between engaging in their various activities and *talking about* those activities, between writing a poem and writing a paper on poetry in general. Philosophers have envied others their right to engage unselfconsciously in their enterprises. In recent times, especially, they have sought to develop an analogous distinction between philosophy as an activity and "meta-philosophy"—as it is sometimes abusively called. And they enjoy describing themselves as *doing* philosophy; they think of philosophy as something one *does* rather than as something one *has* or *believes* or *studies*.

1

This is not, however, quite so available a strategy as it first appears. To begin with, the question of the nature of philosophy, in contrast with the question of the nature, say, of physics, is, unfortunately, an internal question. It might be argued that, since the external questions regarding the natures of all the other disciplines are, in fact, internal questions of philosophy—the definition of the nature of science or of art is not a scientific or artistic problem, but a philosophical problem—why should the external question of the nature of philosophy itself not be an *internal* question of philosophy too? And if philosophy is not to treat of it, what discipline is? So it is not as though one could so readily distinguish between doing philosophy and talking about philosophy. There are ways of talking about philosophy which just *are* philosophy, even if there are other ways which are not. But then it is far from plain that the nature of philosophy is not a philosophical problem if the nature of disciplines in general constitutes philosophical problems. Unfortunately this argument, insofar as it is compelling at all, turns against itself rather savagely. Let us suppose that the nature of philosophy is an internal question of philosophy, so that it is part of philosophical activity to provide some sort of answer to it. Still, it is only one of the *many* internal problems of philosophy. There is no reason, then, why any priority need be assigned it. So those who think of philosophy as an activity may practice that activity in good conscience, without needing to apply it to the special philosophical question of the nature of that activity itself.

Surely it must be by a rather special, ruthless, act of will that this question is held to one side, or ignored in favor of other questions. For it remains a striking fact that there should be a discipline the nature of which is a problem internal to itself. It is almost a defining trait of philosophy that its own existence is a problem internal to itself. I do not mean to suggest that we can not find there to be other disciplines of which something like this might not be true. Rather, I should like to say that when the question of one's nature is part of one's nature, one is not being true to one's nature by ignoring that question. Here, perhaps, an analogy might be helpful. When we try to think seriously about what it is to be essentially *human*, or what is the nature of man as such—and this is hardly a question which a reflective man can avoid—we must recognize that it is almost the very posing of this question, as much as any special answer to it, which, when we take into consideration everything that has to be true in order for such a question to be posed, is distinctive and perhaps even definitory of man. We have been given, of course, some famous, silly answers: man is a featherless biped (Plato) or (somewhat more sympathetically) a rational animal (Aristotle). While these answers cannot satisfy anyone for very long—they are too "external"—the fact remains that the *question itself*, to which they are meant to be sincere answers, is almost by way of being its own answer, especially when we consider what must be the case in order that such a question actually be asked: for the question is reflexive. It is asked by a special type of entity about itself, the entity being special through the fact that it has become an object for itself. And having become an object for itself, it has achieved a *certain distance* from itself. This distance is now logically incorporated into its own structure in such a manner that any answer to the question posed must henceforward take into account this internalized distance. Thus it is characteristic of men that they are conscious of themselves as men. There are certain concepts distinguished through the fact that consciousness of their application is part of the nature of that to which the concept applies. And I believe that the concept of a human being, or a *person*, is of this sort. A person is an entity complex to the degree that his awareness of himself as a certain sort of entity is a component in the sort of thing he is aware of being: he is awakened to his own nature to the extent of wondering what that nature is. And while the fact of his wonderment cannot be the whole of a satisfactory response to itself, it is a crucial element of any satisfactory response. Nobody would, in the end, be satisfied in having as an answer to the question of what they really are, the response that they are the sort of creature who wants an answer to the question they just have asked. But any answer which failed to take into account, or which was flatly incompatible with the considerations of internalized distance which the putting of the question presupposes, would be immediately ruled out as unsatisfactory. Hence the ineptness of the "featherless biped" answer and the rather questionable status of the "rational animal" answer, the latter depending for its acceptability upon some further refinement in the concept of rationality, viz., whether rationality entails this sort of self-querying possibility or is merely compatible with it.

In a similar way, that its own nature is one of its internal problems is not so much a solution to the problem of what philosophy is, as it is a datum which any solution to it must accommodate. But it serves nevertheless quite usefully here as a negative criterion, in that it rules out any characterization of philosophy which is in fact a characterization of a discipline whose nature is *not* an internal problem for itself. And in particular, since the sciences are by common consent admitted to be this latter sort, a final definition of philosophy which did not differentiate it from the sciences as a class must, through this fact, be deemed inadequate. This is perhaps an important consideration, given the rather well-known fact that from its very inception in ancient times, philosophy was never clearly distinguished from the special sciences—the early philosophers having been astronomers or doctors or mathematicians, who never perhaps supposed there was any essential difference between these activities and those others which in fact have earned them a place in the history of philosophy. And this has no doubt stood in the way of getting a satisfactory answer to the self-querying question I am taking as crucial in philosophy, and has perhaps even inhibited it from being grasped as a question which needed posing at all. As it does to each of us individually, self-consciousness comes late to philosophy: historically, I think, only in very recent times has it been really possible to see philosophy as an activity of a special sort, different from the sciences.

2. This is connected with a second fact regarding philosophy. It is perhaps too banal a piece of historical information to mention that a great many intellectual disciplines which simply were taken as parts of philosophy—as they well could be since no distinction was made between philosophy as such and the special sciences—detached themselves from the parent discipline and undertook increasingly autonomous developments. So autonomous have these

been that philosophical competence as such is utterly irrelevant in their connection: no one not a trained physicist, and certainly never in the name of some allegedly higher philosophical authority, would dare contest, much less hope seriously to contribute to, the understanding of an internal question of physics. So over time there has been this increasing scientizing of parts of what traditionally had been branches of philosophy; and since so many disciplines, from astronomy and medicine at the beginning, to mathematics and logic more recently, have gone their ways, there must appear to be a considerable inductive support for a theory that what remains of philosophy must be merely pre-scientific knowledge. And it is not at all implausible to think of aesthetics, or ethics, to take two disciplines still commonly covered in the normal philosophical curriculum, as someday overcoming their retrograde inertia to develop, in accordance with their proper fulfillment, into true sciences. Indeed, many philosophers in the so-called Naturalist school of thought, which dominated American philosophy in the early half of this century, made rather considerable efforts in achieving this hoped-for maturity: to get ethics reduced in some fashion to anthropology or to assimilate the problems of the theory of knowledge in some manner to psychology.

Doubtless there are, and for a considerable time there will remain, pockets of merely pre-scientific thought which pass muster as philosophy. The question of immediate interest, however, is whether the *whole* of philosophy is, in this respect, merely retarded science, and, if it is *not*, then what could it be? In this question there lies implicit, of course, a commitment to science as the paradigm intellectual activity. And along with accepting this paradigm, there goes an argument to the effect that, if not science, then philosophy must be some order of nonsense: pretty nonsense perhaps, if done by masters of language (like Santayana or Plato), stodgy nonsense in the hand of the typical philosophical prosist, but nonsense at whatever level of elegance. This abrupt alternation between science and nonsense depends upon considerations of how, in the most general manner in which we may describe this, scientific propositions are to be understood. Roughly (and there is no need at this point to aim for great precision), the theory here is this: to understand a sentence is (with one important class of exceptions) to know what facts will make it true. The class of exceptions is made up of sentences which may be known to be true merely through their being correctly understood, as would be the case, for example, if the sentence were a definition or logically dependent in a certain way upon a definition. Consider "Every widow has at least one dead husband." One can, of course, set up a search for a woman's husband, but if you do so, you are doubting that she really is a widow, not doubting that widows have dead husbands. For the latter we know to be true merely through understanding what it is to be a widow, and so no appeal to facts, but only appeal to meaning, is required for knowledge that the sentence is true. Or at least understanding suffices for assuring us that the sentence cannot be *false*. Now understanding and knowledge are distinct enough ordinarily, that we are able to understand a sentence *s* without knowing whether it is true or false. So that, in at least the typical case, the understanding of *s* on the part of an individual does not entail his knowing *s* to be true. And this, in part, is because the truth of a sentence is very seldom determined by its meaning. Our characterization of the sentences of science does not require that we know them in fact to be true, but only that we understand them. Understanding requires only that we know what factors would make the sentence true if it were true, and not that we know whether these factors hold. Against the background of this exceedingly permissive criterion of a scientific sentence, we may now ask whether *philosophical* sentences are meaningful in the sense laid down. In other words, we are asking whether, in order to understand a philosophical sentence, we must not know what facts would make it true, and hence whether the ascertainment of philosophical knowledge must not involve just the same sort of fact-finding methods plainly employed in the sciences. If so, then, from the point of view of this very accommodating criterion, can we not say that the sentences of philosophy are scientific? Perhaps the criterion is too elastic, but if philosophical sentences are not scientific by *this* criterion, then it is difficult to see that they should be meaningful at all. Unless, of course, they may be settled merely by appeal to meanings, in which case no fact external to themselves appears relevant to the determination of their truth, so that they then are factually irrelevant, or empty of content. If this broad but plausible criterion is accepted, then the sentences of philosophy, if not empty, either are scientific or are nonsense.

I have endeavored to make my argument sufficiently weak and general for it to exert the pressure we demand of it. Thus it is sometimes argued that a sentence is meaningful only if we can say what *experiences* would verify it. This is a stronger claim by far than I am making. I ask only that we let *s* be meaningful providing that *s* can be made true or false by facts, whether we know what it would be like to *experience* whatever makes a sentence true or not. The stronger argument is more exciting because more vulnerable than mine, but I want a criterion sufficiently broad to support the claim that the sentences of philosophy, if not either empty or nonsense, might be regarded as nascent science. And surely the weakest and least controversial claim one might make regarding science is that the sentences of science should be made true or false by some fact, and that to understand a scientific sentence is to know what fact(s) would make it true. If this is all we should demand of a sentence in order that it be scientific, must not the sentences of philosophy qualify? The criterion, plainly, does not take us very far towards an appreciation, much less a deep understanding, of science as we know it. But let this be our characterization of science, even so.

We have an argument, however, in Section 1, that any characterization of philosophy which does not mark the difference between philosophy and science has to be *inadequate*. It follows, then, that if the above should be our characterization of science, philosophy cannot, consistently with our former argument, satisfy *it*. So the former argument, together with this very weak criterion, forces us to conclude that the sentences of philosophy are either empty or nonsense.

Dismal as it may sound, I am not loath to acquiesce in this conclusion. But before utterly yielding to it, let us ask how broadly the notion of a fact is to be taken. Scientific sentences, let us say, are made true by facts, whatever we may want to say regarding the nature of facts as such. The question only is whether the sentence that scientific sentences are made true by facts, is *itself* a scientific sentence? Well, one may want to say: *it is a fact* that scientific sentences are made true by facts. But surely, the sentence that they are so is not in answer to any *internal* questions of science: it rather says something external regarding the sentences of science quite in general. So *it* cannot be a scientific sentence, all scientific sentences being answers to internal questions of the sciences. If, however, it is made true by a fact, it has to be, by our weak criterion, a scientific sentence. So we get an incoherent result when we apply our two notions to the *very sentence* which was to specify that about the sciences which required that philosophy either be science or something empty or nonsensical. Why then *should* we acquiesce in the consequence? Since the argument which means to establish it must, by its own criterion, either be nonsense or be empty? Perhaps we can dissolve the incoherency by reconsidering more carefully the notion of a fact. Perhaps, at least, it is through a fact of a different kind from the facts which make scientific sentences true that this statement *about* scientific sentences is made true? I applaud this suggestion. But notice that the task of differentiating different *orders* or *types* of fact cannot be an internal scientific question, especially when one of the orders of fact to be identified is that order of fact which makes scientific sentences true. But it *is* a question internal to the discipline concerned with this specific task. So again, this discipline cannot be scientific since its own nature *is* an internal question for it. This, however, is very close to our notion of philosophy, which exhibits a curious trait in that it cannot be talking about the sciences without talking about *itself*, cannot say what is so of science as a whole without taking a stand outside of science and insofar identifying a difference between it and what it is talking about. If this were generalized, it might be concluded that the definition of philosophy is part of every philosophical problem: philosophy is defining itself whenever it defines anything at all. Well, this would be a deep result. But it would then seriously raise the question whether there is a separate problem of defining philosophy. Might it not now be that in *doing philosophy*, whatever our problem, we *are*, after all, *showing* what philosophy is? So that the way to define philosophy just is to do philosophy?

3. I believe a provisional answer to this somewhat rhetorical question can be coaxed out of our discussion thus far. Consider once more the sentence: *Scientific sentences are made true or false by facts.* Without pausing to consider just now what facts are, let us examine a specimen scientific sentence: "Water freezes at 32° Fahrenheit." We all understand this sentence in a rough way. It means that any sample of water which attains this temperature freezes; and it is *made true* by actual samples of water freezing when they reach this temperature. The sentence is about water, temperature, and the freezing state: it is a sentence about reality: about the *world.* But our sentence—which says that the class of sentences, of which this sentence about water is a member, is made true by facts—*our* sentence is not about the world in this sense. Nor, strictly speaking, is it a sentence just about this class of sentences. It is, if about anything, about the *connection between* that class of sentences and the world. It is about the space between scientific language, which is the language made up of sentences which are true or false, and the world, which makes those sentences true or false. So, if our sentence is made true by a fact, this fact is not, like the fact which makes the sentence about water true, a part of the world. Rather, to speak dramatically, it is a fact which contains the world as part of *it*, but only part. The other part is language. So, to continue in this somewhat gnomic idiom, the sentence that scientific sentences are made true by facts is perpendicular to the world and to sentences about the world. It is, in this respect, empty. It is so because it is not made true by any feature of the world, being, as it were, an *external* statement about the world. But it is not empty in the way in which "All widows have at least one dead husband" is empty. The latter is made true by a rule of language. In saying this, we are making an external statement about language.

If this intuition is correct, it follows that the habitat of philosophy is the curious interspace between language and the world. This would explain the frustration which critics of philosophy have felt when they sought from philosophy, usually, if not inevitably, in vain for interesting facts or information concerning the world. It is, if you wish, not in the nature of philosophy to contribute to our primary knowledge of the world. Philosophy cannot add to our knowledge, at least in the sense in which it is paradigmatically the function of science to do this. Contrasted with this function, philosophy must be regarded as inherently empty. Here, once again, an analogy with consciousness might be helpful. To be *conscious* of the world is not to add anything to that of which one is conscious. We are, rather, inclined to suppose that the world would be there, just as it is, whether we were conscious of it as there or not: that the world is independent of our consciousness of it. Its existence does not in any way *depend* upon our consciousness of it, but our consciousness of it depends upon *it*. Consciousness is a secondary and derivative thing. So it is, in a way, with philosophy. Philosophy is a discipline of disciplines. It has, in the sense in which the primary disciplines have a subject matter, no subject matter of its own. So the various disciplines could be just as they are without philosophy, but philosophy would be nothing without them. So in a way (but only in a way) it is secondary and derivative. But the expression "a discipline of disciplines" is misleading in the characterizations it suggests; it suggests an arrogant one: disciplining in the sense of ruling over and prescribing for the separate primary disciplines, exacting compliance with its higher-order strictures: the old, self-congratulatory view of philosophy as "queen of the sciences." It also suggests a humble one: the self-abasing view of philosophy as hand-maiden to the sciences, taking its order from the sciences, executing the tasks of conceptual housekeeping they are too robustly busy to tend to themselves.

4. This latter, hand-maiden view has recently enjoyed a certain acceptance by philosophers themselves, largely in consequence of destructive arguments of the same genre as (though considerably more refined than) the one we employed to show that, if not scientific, the sentences of philosophy must either be empty or nonsense. These destructive tactics were meant to be liberating and

purgative, to free us once and for all from the burden of unresolved problems borne by human intellect from the inception of philosophy.

It was the hope and even, more sanguinely, the boast of those who wielded these destructive arguments, that through them the whole unredeemable mass of philosophical discourse could be relegated to the status of pointless answers to pseudo questions, the vacuity of it all having been concealed by the portentousness and heavy rhetoric with which philosophical language had always been freighted. I am referring here to the celebrated Verifiability criterion of meaningfulness, which, in the eyes of its early proponents, appeared neatly, incontrovertably, and finally to distinguish what is meaningful from what is nonsense—when the latter could not be recognized as such in virtue of being stated in grammatically unexceptionable sentences. The Verifiability criterion, roughly, was this: We understand a sentence when, and only when, we know what *experiences* would verify, or be relevant to the verification of, the sentence. When we cannot say what experiences would verify it, then, unless it is an empty tautology, it has to be meaningless. It seemed very natural to make a further claim, not about meaningfulness but about *meaning*, according to which the meaning of a sentence just is its *mode of verification*. A theory of meaningfulness need not in fact presuppose any specific theory of meaning, but the absence of any mode of verifying a sentence seemed quite plainly to constitute a description of exactly the conditions under which we might want to say that we do not understand a sentence, or that it cannot be understood at all. For we would then have no idea of how to establish any connection between it and the world; and it is difficult therefore to see, if it should pretend to be about the world, what it would be for it to be true or false, or what descriptive force it might have. So if the absence of a mode of verification means the absence of meaning, it is natural to identify its meaning with its mode of verification. It might have some *non*-descriptive force, to be sure. But to retreat to this position is tantamount to accepting the Verifiability criterion. For it never meant to deny that sentences which were descriptively meaningless might have *some* other use or force or purpose than that of describing the world. Well, since philosophers often had thought they *were* trying to say something about the world, to say now that philosophical sentences were meaningful "in some other way" would not be to contest, but to accept the Verifiability criterion. Its claim was that, when taken descriptively, philosophical sentences were nonsense.

The Verifiability criterion was the defining basis of the school of logical positivism. But there is a sympathy between it and the rather earlier philosophical school of pragmatism, which we might pause to consider briefly in this context. The theses of pragmatism may be stated, somewhat vulgarly, thus: (i) to understand a sentence *s* is to know how to use *s* in the organization of experience; (ii) if *s* and *s'* have the same use, they have the same meaning, however they may appear to differ in point of grammar, vocabulary, and the like: a difference that fails to make a difference in practice, is in effect no difference at all; (iii) if a sentence *s* has no practical use, then *s* has no meaning: as Wittgenstein (whose views are, incidentally, not remote from pragmatism's, since he was committed to the thesis that the meaning of a sentence is by and large its use) once said: "a wheel which turns though nothing turns with it, is not part of the machine." To be sure, a sentence may have some *personal* meaning: it may seem to make (at least) some *difference to me* even if it has no otherwise practical use. Such a view was that of William James, who in fact advocated a pair of interesting and characteristically optimistic theses in connection with it: (a) just when a sentence makes no difference in practice, then, in case it happens to make a *difference to me* whether I believe it to be true or not, I have a *right* to believe it; and (b) if I exercise this right, my believing the sentence may contribute to its making an objective difference, may become causally involved in the sentence *becoming true*. Thus, if I believe in the rationality of the universe, my acting in the light of this belief can contribute to the universe's rationality. James appears to have been prepared to say that the meaning of a sentence just is the sentimental difference it makes to him who wishes to believe it. Or at least this will be the case for any proposition not otherwise meaningful by pragmatist criteria, such as when there appears to be no way in which to determine, through using it, whether the sentence is true or not—the pragmatist view being that to call a sentence true is one with saying the sentence has a successful use. But when there *is* no way of using a sentence, it follows that the sentence is meaningless by pragmatist criteria; and the question is whether, in view of this, we could intelligibly believe a meaningless sentence. Perhaps the "difference to me" merely consists in the fact that the sentence causes me to have certain feelings. But James's rather personal interpretation of pragmatic meaning was generally distasteful to his more austere co-doctrinaires, whose view that the meaning of a sentence is its practical consequences—or its consequences in *practice*—is, to revert now to our topic, more exacting a criterion than that of the Verifiability criterion. For the former insists that a sentence actually *make* a difference, that it in fact have an instrumental use. But the verificationists do not demand that a sentence in fact be verified, only that it in principle be verifiable through experience. And they thought this an exceedingly tolerating demand. It excluded certain propositions about Absolutes, about Being-as-such, about Cosmic Souls, and comparable (to them) unintelligible monsters in the menagerie of the metaphysician. But even here, they were prepared to be gracious only providing they knew what they were talking about: and this, they urged, required only that they be told what experiences will or would be relevant to the verification of sentences about these.

5. Pragmatists and verificationists alike held to the scientific sentence as their paradigm. They believed their respective principles of meaningfulness to be but descriptive of actual scientific discourse. And in connection with this, they thought they had found a proper if unexalted role for philosophy. It is not the task of philosophy to frame sentences about the world, unless philosophers decide finally just to transfer to one of the sciences, which would mean the abandonment, not the reform, of philosophy. Rather, philosophy, though not science, is *about* science in a certain way. Thus, it might be asked (as it was) whether the principles of verifiability satisfied their own criteria of meaningfulness and, if not, whether they must not then be nonsense and, as it were,

suicidal victims of their own demands? And here, I think, the verificationists were consonant with their own principles to the extent of saying that their criteria were descriptive of scientific practice; philosophy, as a generalized description of science, is redeemed thereby as a viable, meaningful endeavor: philosophy becomes coincident with philosophy of science, broadly construed.

This may be given, however, a narrow or a broad interpretation, depending upon how we are to construe the notion of the description of science. For many philosophers, it became a matter of very close attention to the structure and history of actual scientific theories: relativity and quantum mechanics, for example, which were having, at the time, immense conceptual repercussions. Yet the activities of philosophers who engaged in these detailed and illuminating studies must be appreciated in a context rather different from that of the sociology or the history of science: they behaved not as biographers ultimately, but as analysts, and their concern may be characterized almost exactly by those terms we have used to characterize philosophy itself. Science has a history, it has an institutional structure and social implications and a code of what constitutes legitimate method. It may thus be studied from the perspective of one or another of the social sciences. But the social sciences are sciences, they are concerned with making certain statements about the world. So construed, the sciences they study are part of the world: it is a fact of history that Newton delivered a theory of universal gravitation to the world in 1672; it is a fact about the world that there are scientists who are changing its physical and social surface. Notice how beguiling, by our criteria, the concept of a *science of science* is! For in talking about science, it is *ipso facto* talking about itself, and hence satisfies our criterion for philosophy, since its own nature seems exactly to be an internal question for itself! So it must seem unavoidable that the science of science is what exactly constitutes an answer to the question of what philosophy is! And notice, too, how this appears to solve the problem of the final remnant of philosophy, of what remains when all the special sciences will have detached themselves and gone their autonomous ways. What is left is the science of science. So our own analysis thus far must seem quite harmonious indeed with the programs of verificationists and pragmatists. But this conclusion is far too abrupt, and is, I think, wrong. Which brings me to the other way in which we must construe the description of science. After discussing that we shall have, I hope, a clearer sense of the difference between the philosophy of science and the science of science, and in general between philosophy and science.

6. Once again, let us think of science in the broadest possible way, as a systematic endeavor to make true statements about the world. Whatever else science may be said to do or to try to do, surely it would be counted a failure if it did not succeed in this. But so broad a characterization permits at least one basic distinction between science and the world. This is not to deny that science is "in the world," that it is "part of the world" in every sense and in every respect other than that which requires an essential contrast between the sentences of science and what they are about, or what confers truth-value upon them. This relationship, *between* science and the world, is not also a relation *within* the world. And so we must distinguish those inquiries concerned with science as part of the world—which may properly be called sciences of science— and those concerned rather with the connection between science and the world—which may properly be called philosophy of science or, for that matter, may just be called philosophy. So again, we emerge with a view that philosophy is essentially located in a space between language and the world, a space which does not exist until, of course, language arises: so that the existence of philosophy is contingent upon the existence of something which stands in the required relation with the world so as to provide a space for philosophy to occupy. In this respect then, we may differentiate a philosophical concern with language from a *linguistic* concern with it. Linguistics is a science, addressed to language where language is considered a natural phenomenon in the world. Philosophy is concerned with language as one term of a relationship, the other term of which is the world which language hopefully describes. And in the end, the world is of *philosophical* interest only so far as *it* is one term in the relationship with language. To be concerned with the world non-relationally is, in the broad sense we have demarcated, to be engaged in a scientific activity.

Now we may offer a general division of the main types of philosophical problems that there are. First, there are problems arising out of language when the latter is considered as one term of the relationship between language and the world. These are problems of meaning and of understanding. Then there are problems concerned with the world, taken as the other term of the relation. These problems arise in connection with specifying the conditions under which language may get a purchase on the world, viz., how must the world be if it is to be intelligibly described. These are questions of metaphysics. Finally there are problems pertaining to the connection between language and the world. These are problems of knowledge and of truth. It is not always simple to talk about one of these sets of problems without bringing in considerations which bear upon the others, but keeping these grand divisions in mind, we may now begin to discuss in some measure of detail certain sets of problems of each sort.

II ← UNDERSTANDING

7. The difficulty of discussing one set of philosophical problems without bringing in implicit reference to another set may be seen already in the two theories of meaningfulness discussed above. Thus, still speaking crudely, the Verifiability principle holds a sentence s to be meaningful just in case, when not a tautology, it is verifiable. Verifying would ordinarily be understood as having some (sense) experience which would verify, or provide some basis for believing s to be true. Now though ostensibly this is a proposition concerning meaningfulness, it makes an implicit reference to the concept of experience, in that, to understand a sentence is here taken to be more or less one with being able to say what *experiences* would verify it; and this in turn presupposes that one more or less should *know* one were having those experiences when one had them. Questions of understanding thus lead into questions of knowledge, and of truth: for to specify under what conditions a sentence is verified is one with specifying under what conditions it may be taken as true or as likely to be true. To be sure, one can understand a sentence independently of knowing whether it is true or not, just as a sentence may be meaningful independently of whether it is true. Accordingly, then, understanding and meaning are independent, respectively, of knowledge and truth. Nevertheless, definitions of meaning and of understanding often, and perhaps inevitably, make implicit reference to conceptual features of knowledge and truth. Finally, of course, the concept of experience itself requires amplification: what must we experience in order to be able to say whether a sentence is verified or not? Do we

experience things? Or aspects of things? Or what? And this turns us back to the question of the meaning of the sentence, viz., whether for it to be verified, it is actually required that the objects of experience be of a certain sort. These conceptual entanglements and cross references suggest the systematic character of philosophy, and they moreover imply the difficult consequence that much as we should like to be able to work piecemeal at philosophical questions, it is not likely we shall get answers to any of them without getting (or presupposing) answers to all. And if nothing else, it must alert us to the extreme care which must be exercised in philosophical thinking, in order not to move involuntarily off onto a spur so close and so parallel to the one along which we think we are advancing, that we believe ourselves to have entered upon exceedingly complicated territory when in fact we are merely lost. Success in philosophical thinking is to be attained only by adhering to these twin demands of keeping the totality in mind and the elements distinct. With this in mind, let us commence to explore the topic of meaning from a philosophical point of view.

8. I shall designate as a *meaning-vehicle* any fragment of the world which is taken to bear a meaning. This will include words, sentences, names, ideas, concepts, even pictures. Without attempting a general characterization of meaning, let us mark off a special, if rather crucial, kind of meaning which I shall speak of as *descriptive meaning*. A sentence has, for example, a descriptive meaning when it sensibly can be supposed to be either true or false. Questions, thus, do not have descriptive meaning (though the answers to some of them do), nor do imperatives. Neither "Shut that door!" nor "Is that door shut?" is true, nor is either of them false. Let us say that the descriptive meaning of a sentence *s* is a rule which specifies under what conditions *s* is true. Obviously, *s* will have that meaning even when false, i.e., even when the conditions specified by the rule do not hold. So one may say that the meaning of *s* is *invariant with regard to changes in the truth-value of s*. Thus, to understand *s* is to know under what conditions *s* would be true. But since *s* can be either true or false without any change in meaning, even the perfect understanding of *s* will not in general guarantee that ones *knows* that *s* is true. Understanding is

distinct from knowledge, as meaning is distinct from, or independent of, truth.

Sentences are not by any means the only bearers of descriptive meaning. Let us consider pictures. Imagine a picture of a girl gazing out a window. Anyone who has mastered the not very complicated conventions of pictorial representation can understand such a picture. He is able directly to say what the picture is *about*. But in addition to understanding, he may wish to know who the girl is, or where and when the scene depicted on canvas in fact took place. Consonant with our understanding, we must appreciate the artist's reply that the picture is purely imaginary, that there is no such girl, that it is all "made up," that it is a fantasy or a dream in paint. We may say that the picture has just the meaning it has, invariant as to whether there is any actual girl or window which it specifically represents. Pictures, then, are analogous to sentences in this respect, and one could easily extend the notion of truth-and-falsity to apply to pictures. Let us, instead of this, speak of pictures as *representing* or *not-representing*, invariant as to the meaning of pictures, and, to understand a picture is to know what conditions must be satisfied in order for a picture to represent. And now let us say that, like *truth* and *falsity*, *represents* and *not-represents* are examples of pairs of *semantical values*. This way, we can let each sort of meaning-vehicle have the kind of semantical value appropriate to it. Thus, a concept may have instances or be empty, all the while remaining just the concept that it is. We understand the concept of unicorns whether there are unicorns or not, i.e., whether there are instances to which the concept applies or not. So "true," "represents," "has instances," will be examples of semantical values, or rather, as we might say, *positive* semantical values, since the opposite of each of these is a semantical value as well. We may now say generally that the descriptive meaning of a meaning-vehicle is given by a rule which specifies the conditions under which it bears the positive semantical value appropriate to it.

9. It becomes a question of extreme philosophical importance to determine which meaning-vehicles have descriptive meaning and, in case they do, whether their essential meaning is exhausted

by such descriptive meaning as they may have. A crucial case arises in connection with moral terms, and their use in such sentences as "*x* is good" or "*y* is right." There is a widely held analysis of these terms according to which, when we use them in their primary sense, we are *not* stating some fact about whatever we say is (for example) good, we are *not* saying anything which is true or false, but rather we are executing some action by means of these terms: we are *commending* rather than describing; or we are *enjoining* others to adopt a certain attitude; or we are *expressing* a feeling towards, rather than saying something true (or false) about, these things. These views exemplify what is called non-cognitivism. It is the view of the non-cognitivist that sentences employing moral predicates are not primarily descriptive, and hence do not primarily express knowledge. It is, accordingly, a fundamental mistake to set about looking for some such properties as goodness or rightness, a mistake essentially due to our taking the sentences which use the appropriate terms as predicating goodness (say) of some object when in fact the sentence has some different use altogether. But non-cognitivism in ethical theory is but one of a class of non-cognitivisms, or non-descriptivisms, as we might term them, since it is always crucial to determine whether a term which appears to have a certain philosophical importance is actually descriptive. There has in recent times been a wholesale endeavor to deprecate the importance of descriptive meaning altogether. Thus there are views according to which "true" itself is not a descriptive term, and others according to which when a man uses the words "I know" he is not saying but rather *doing* something: is giving his word rather than reporting a fact about himself. One can think of language in a purely instrumental way, so that the meaning of a sentence would be its use in communication or manipulation. This was a thesis regarding meaning which is notoriously associated with the later philosophy of Wittgenstein, a thesis amounting to a non-cognitivist view of language almost as a whole. This in turn goes with a certain conception of man as a user of language. It sees man as an agent, practically implicated in a form of life with which he is one, a view which contrasts sharply with another and dominating philosophical view of man, standard since at least Descartes, which sees man as a knower rather than a doer, concerned to describe a world he is set over against, a lonely intellect not even certain that there is a society with which to communicate or a world in which it might exist. But with this shift from Descartes to Wittgenstein (and, before him, John Dewey), whole classes of philosophical problems dissolve away or refuse to arise, so much so that Wittgenstein felt he could credit himself with having *ended* philosophy, though his achievement would at best have been an abandonment of certain classes of traditional problems through a weakening of the grip of descriptive meaning as the paradigmatic sort of meaning. So there is, in effect, a deep struggle between Wittgenstein and his followers, on the one side, and the philosophical tradition on the other, as to which parts of language are to be treated as primarily descriptive. And obviously, the line allegedly separating ethical discourse from discourse in general can be erased by either of two extreme measures: by treating ethical predicates as descriptive, or by regarding *no* terms as descriptive, but all of them, rather, as subserving some instrumental function in the conduct of life. These are extremes, of course, and Wittgenstein did not himself go so far as to denounce descriptivity altogether. Yet there remains this contest in contemporary philosophy: it is as though there were two opposed and utterly irreconcilable views of language, and hence of man and his connection with the world, and hence of philosophy itself, which we have defined as being occupied with the connection between language and the world. Of course there is room for a kind of dualism, as we might term it here, an uneasy but very likely sane acceptance of the proposition that the whole of discourse is not to be assimilated to either of these radical extremes, and that certain meaning-vehicles are irreducibly non-descriptive ("meaningless" if one takes, as the logical positivists once did, descriptive meaning as the *whole* of meaning). But with this dualism there is opportunity for raids and forays into enemy territory on either side of what must be an essentially fluid line. A great deal of current philosophizing seems best appreciated in these terms: as a kind of grinding, interminable trench warfare, where brief and indecisive engagements are possible, and no clear hope of any final, total victory. The image is perhaps over-dramatic, yet one cannot overemphasize the degree to which philosophical controversies can in the end be viewed as a controversy over the limits of descriptive meaningfulness.

10. Even should the issue be decided in favor of descriptivity in any given case, it is not as though a satisfyingly final philosophical clarity will have been achieved. Consider, once again, characteristic moral terms, e.g., "good" in "*x* is good." It is difficult to broach the matter here without usurping questions pertaining to the theory of knowledge and to metaphysics, as much as to the theory of understanding; but many philosophers have wanted to argue that "*x* is good" is true when, and only when, *x* has a certain property, namely goodness, in exactly the same way in which "*x* is yellow" is true when, and only when, *x* has the property of yellowness. Now concerning (at least) yellow, the following may be plausibly said: (i) commonly, nothing tells us that something is yellow apart from the fact that we see it to be so, so that (ii) there is ordinarily no property, distinct from yellow itself, by means of which we know something to be yellow, and in which yellowness itself partly consists. As things stand, (iii) yellow can be regarded as a simple property, in the respect that it is not resolvable, or analyzable, into anything more elementary in which it consists; *it itself* is what it consists in, to put it bluntly. In case "good" is logically similar to "yellow," then, on this argument, nothing tells us that something is good except the fact that it is so, and we must, accordingly, know that something is good in just the way in which we normally know that something is yellow, viz., there must be some moral intuition similar to seeing. And, moreover, goodness must be a simple, unanalyzable property of things, not itself resoluble into simpler constituents; in consequence, the term "good" is not definable by means of any simpler constituents: there is nothing, distinct from the property of goodness, which tells us with certainty that something is good. This is a view of G. E. Moore, who used it in an attack on what he characterized as Naturalism in ethical theory, the theory which, as he saw it, proposed to define goodness in terms of some "natural" property such as pleasure, utility, or some such thing. Goodness not being any such natural property, Moore concluded that it must then be a *non-natural* one; and though we can examine here neither his arguments for this nor their consequences, we must pause to distinguish at least three different things which the notion of simplicity might mean. (i) There are terms, the meaning of which must commonly be taught via ostension, that is to say, a man commonly is said to have learned the meaning of certain terms by being presented with things to which these terms apply. This contrasts with learning the meaning of terms through some sort of definition. If there are terms which can *only* be taught through ostension, then these are simple from the *point of view of meaning*. (ii) Does it follow, from the fact that a term is simple relative to the theory of meaning, that a man only can *know* that something is an instance of that term directly, that is to say, non-inductively? It may be so. Or it may better be supposed that we can conclusively verify that something is an instance only by directly knowing that it is so, that is, not by knowing on the basis of some evidence, but on the basis of directly apprehending the thing to be an instance of that to which the simple term applies. This would then be simplicity from the point of view of *knowledge*. (iii) Does it follow from the fact that a term may be simple in both or either of the two senses just marked, that that to which it applies must be *simple as such*? Suppose, thus, that 'yellow' is a simple term from both points of view: must it be simple in any deeper sense? That there should be simples in this *last* sense would be a theory about what the *world* is made up of. This is simplicity from the point of view of *being*. These senses of simplicity respectively pertain to our primitive *concepts*, our basic *knowledge*, and the fundamental entities of the world.

Moore evidently regarded good as simple in all three senses, and all we can afford to ask here is whether they are logically implicated with one another. But I don't believe that if something is simple in one sense it *must* be simple in the other two senses. It is independently arguable, perhaps, that some terms must be simple in that not every term can be defined. It is similarly arguable that not everything can be known on the basis of evidence, but that some things have to be known directly. But it does not follow from these two facts that there have to be simples in the deep sense, although it *might* follow that, if there are simples in this last, deep sense, then the terms which apply to these might have to be simple in the first two senses. But I do not think it does follow. The simples of the universe might, for example, be utterly inaccessible to direct knowledge, and the terms which apply to them could not be taught ostensively since the simples might be utterly inaccessible to observation, and so the meanings would have to be taught only through mastering a rather complicated theory. In order to get the three sorts of simplicity to be logically impli-cated with one another, we have to introduce a further thesis.

11. *Empiricism* is the theory that there are basic simple terms, the meaning of which can only be taught through *experiencing* instances of things to which these terms (correctly) apply. But rather a stronger claim than this would be made by the typical classical empiricist: namely, that any descriptive term we under-stand is either simple in this sense or else is exhaustively definable by means of some set of terms which are simple in this sense. The great originating empiricist philosophers—Locke, Berkeley, Hume, and Mill—thought in terms of *ideas* rather than words; they held that there are simple ideas and compound ideas, and that com-pound ideas are resoluble without remainder into some set of simple ideas; and their theory may be sloganized as the view that there are no simple ideas in the mind not caused by some specific sense experience which the idea resembles. Compound ideas need not have been caused as such in this manner, it being here that the empiricists left room for the work of imagination, viz., imagination can assemble but not create simple ideas. Now the idea of an ultimate simple which we cannot experience might be an unin-telligible notion to the empiricist. If it is meaningful, then either it must be compound or directly experienceable. With some such thesis, we could connect our notions of simplicity with one another. For the empiricists, then, ideas rather than terms would be the bearers of meaning, and while this in fact gives rise to a number of exceedingly complicated questions, the essential

structure of empiricist theories of understanding is not much affected by a decision to talk about understanding simple terms, or understanding simple ideas. In either case, what empiricism amounts to is a certain theory of *learning*, that is, a theory of *how we come to understand*, or, in a metaphorical way, how the mind gets stocked with its contents. Locke thus used it as an attack on the proposal that there are *innate ideas*, insisting that the mind, antecedent to specific episodes of sense experience, must be a blank tablet. Hume supposed there *could* be some exceptions to this, though not any innate ideas as such: I could be caused to have the ideas of a color I had never experienced in case I had experienced colors precisely adjacent to it in the same continuous color band with a gap in place of the color I would ordinarily come to have the idea of by experiencing *it*. As a theory of the causation of ideas (or of understanding), however, empiricism is vulnerable to the logical possibility that our ideas might be caused in some way other than by sensing as ordinarily construed, and that we might understand whatever we in fact understand though we did not *in fact* learn any of it via experience. Since empiricism, in its classical form, is a causal theory, it is subject to whatever skepticism causal theories as such may be liable. Bertrand Russell once proposed that it is logically possible that the entire universe could have come into existence five minutes ago, stocked with everything just as it is, including us and all our memories and nostalgias. No one seriously supposes it did so, but it is not a logical impossibility, and, insofar as it is not, it is not logically impossible that none of our ideas should have been caused in the manner proposed by the empiricists. If Russell's hypothesis were factually correct, and the universe five minutes old, we would have *learned* the meaning of very few terms indeed, though we would understand whatever we now in fact, on the present view which assigns a reasonable stability to the causal laws and a reasonable duration to the universe, understand. The question then becomes one of whether we can be caused to understand through other means than through learning. Thus if by taking some pill we could become masters of the differential calculus, the result would be the same as if we had learned it, but colleges might be replaced with pharmacies. So in the end, however interesting empiricism may be in its classical form, it is not so much a theory of understanding as it is a theory of learning, and so belongs less to philosophy than to science. Within a theory of learning, however, it might very well be true that, unless at least some terms were learned in the way proposed by empiricism, no terms could be understood at all. This is a weaker, perhaps, but for that reason more defensible, version of empiricism. But I shall not pursue it here.

Let us shift back from questions of learning to questions of understanding, *whatever* may be the causes of understanding. And let us revert to our earlier notion that, to understand the meaning of a meaning-vehicle is to have mastered a rule which specifies under what conditions it receives the positive semantical value appropriate to it. According to this, to understand the term "red" is to be master of a rule under which "*a* is red" would be true. To understand, in whatever way that we do so, is to know what it would be like to experience something as red. That there should be a class of such terms, and that these terms should be basic in some way, may now be taken as a modified empiricism. So revamped, it specifies a set of conditions not so much under which we would have understanding, but rather under which we would have knowledge. To understand "*a* is red" is to be in a position to determine when "*a* is *red*" is true, and it is at least arguable that there could be no episode of the latter sort of knowledge without an actual experience of something red.

The problem now is only whether there is some way other than actually experiencing red by which one could know that "*a* is red" is true: could a blind man, for example, know this sentence to be true? Could he not, for example, merely know it to be true by asking someone reliable? And hence on the basis of evidence? So he might. But the possibility would seriously remain that if the blind man so understands the concept of red that the only way in which he can know that "*a* is red" is true is through evidence (and never directly), that he has not mastered the rule for understanding "red" at all. We, who are sighted, may at times know that something is red by evidence. We do so because there are cases where, say, the shape of a bird is a flat silhouette against the sky, and yet, knowing that birds with that shape are always red, we know this bird to be red via inference. But such inference depends upon laws connecting shapes with colors, and the *establishment* of such laws would surely require the *direct* possibility of establishing "*a* is red." For unless things are directly identifiable, they are not capable of correlation. But a blind man is then incapable of establishing correlations of the required sort, hence incapable of knowing indirectly, viz., on the basis of evidence, that something is red. This argument, if persuasive, would entail that the blind cannot understand the meaning of color terms, and cannot because they cannot tell what red *looks* like.

It might be supposed that there are blind men who know what red looks like, but can never tell—because they cannot see—when something is red. So, though they would be masters of the rule, they cannot apply it. There was at one time some considerable speculation about the closely connected Molyneaux problem, which was the problem of what a blind man restored to sight would at first experience. If it were logically possible even for the congenitally blind to know what red looks like, then, short of adopting some exceedingly farfetched theory such as that of the transmigration of souls, the empiricist theory of learning would again be false. I cannot say whether such a case ever does arise. But would we find it absurd that a blind man, restored to sight, should be able, without any hesitation, to say: that is red, when presented with a red object, and add: it looks just the way I knew it would? Suppose we could equip him with this knowledge by causing a change in his brain. This would not be *teaching*, nor *learning*, but he would have the knowledge, though without experience.

12. Taken as a theory of learning, empiricism would have been committed to a theory of meaning for those terms (or those simple ideas) which could only be understood through sense-learning. The meanings of these terms would have to be the very things to which the term applied, so that the meaning of "red" would be the class of red things, in that, if we did not have access through our senses to the members of this class, the term would be meaningless to us. Thus a patch of color would be the meaning of a term, or part of the meaning since, of course, the assumption is that no one would take the term "red" to be the proper name of the particular patch of red in connection with which he learned the meaning of the term: he must generalize, as it were, to the class of red things, and realize that the term itself applies equally and indifferently to each and to all instances. This of course entails that the world contains meanings (since colors now are meanings), a view felt to be reprehensible by certain philosophers, notably Wittgenstein: for him, meanings are not things, and the world consists solely of things. So it may. But nobody would be pretending that the world, *in addition* to the ordinary things it contains—stars and oysters, garters and girls—contains meanings: rather, that these very things are the meanings, or parts of the meanings, of "oyster," "star," etc.

Let us put this more abstractly now. Consider any term *t* which has (noncontroversially) descriptive meaning. Then there are two ways in which we might speak of the meaning of *t*. By (a) specifying the rule which in turn specifies the conditions under which "*x* is a *t*" is true or by (b) specifying the class of things to which *t* correctly applies. But suppose that class is empty? A man may understand the term "bird" in that he knows under what conditions "*x* is a bird" would be true: but, unless the term is basic and empiricism is a correct theory of learning, he can understand this whether or not there are things to which the term correctly applies, e.g., in case "*x* is a bird" were always false, the way "x is a unicorn," is. Some such distinction is fundamental in philosophy: logicians traditionally distinguished between the *extension* of a term, viz., the class of things to which the term applies, and the *intension* of the term, which is variously described as the *concept* which the term is connected with, or the *idea* the term connotes, or some such thing. And surely, some distinction of the sort is crucial enough: when we think of the meaning of a term as its extension exclusively, as would be the primitive temptation, then terms with empty extensions would be meaningless—a consequence particularly vexing when we make something like the same sort of analysis for *sentential* meaning, e.g., we might think of the meaning of a sentence as that state of affairs in the world to which the sentence applies. Then a sentence with an "empty extension" would be meaningless—from which consequence the appalling inference was drawn by the Sophist Protagoras that there are no false sentences which are meaningful. There are none because, to say that a sentence is false is to say that there is nothing in the world it applies to, and, if meaningfulness requires that there be such a thing in the world, no sentence can be meaningful and false. But, since we understand putatively false sentences, they cannot be false. This is the basis of his famous *homo mensura* doctrine, according to which each man is the measure of all things. One of the chief philosophical tasks undertaken by Socrates was to establish the possibility of meaningful but false sentences.

These considerations encourage the view that the meaning of a sentence *cannot* be what the sentence applies to when it is true. Attempts have been made to develop purely extensional theories of meaning in recent times, but this is not the place to discuss them. The motives for undertaking such programs are, as it happens, largely metaphysical. This requires a few words of comment. Let us think broadly of meaning-vehicles as we have. Names, words, sentences, concepts, pictures, may each have meaning in both of the senses we have specified. In order to make this plain let us distinguish between *reference* and *meaning*, to use a pair of terms introduced by Frege, so that the reference of a vehicle will be that in the world which the vehicles stands for: the actual person George Washington for the name "George Washington," the class of goats for the term "goat." Since reference may fail without a vehicle being rendered meaningless (except in the possibly exceptional case of names which, as Mill once argued, may *only* refer) the meaning has to be distinct from the things, whatever they may be, to which a vehicle is supposed to refer. But then this leaves the question moot as to what meanings are; and, for reasons not dissimilar to those referred to a moment ago in connection with Wittgenstein, there is a reluctance to countenance the existence of whatever curious entities meanings might be. This then encourages the enterprise of developing purely referential (or extensional) theories of meaning. With the success of such enterprises I shall not be concerned; but the theory advanced here, according to which a meaning is a *rule*, may be sufficiently uncompromising, metaphysically, to be accepted even by the most nominalistic philosophers.

13. A theory of meaning, or of understanding, has of course to provide some account of what it is for two vehicles to have the *same* meaning. This is a rather more crucial matter than most nonphilosophers would spontaneously suppose. It is perhaps best brought out by thinking of certain elementary substitutions one might make in a scientific formula. Thus we might say that in physics we have such terms as mass (m), length (l), and time (t), by means of which other terms may be defined. Thus velocity is l/t; acceleration (a) is l/t^2; force (F) is ma. This means that we can replace these expressions with one another without any change in the truth value of the contexts within which the interchange is effected: if a formula containing a is true, replacing a with l/t^2 should not make it false. But this can be assured when, and only when, the replacing expressions may be said to have the same meaning. In view of this one might propose, as a criterion for two vehicles to have the same reading, that they should be mutually interchangeable in an identical context without alteration of semantical value. If they have the same meaning we must know in advance that this may be effected; but it is at least a fair *test* to attempt to find a context in which replacement of a with b induces a change, thus showing, unless the change in semantical value can be explained away in some other fashion, that the terms are not synonymous. Such a test was employed over and over by Socrates in the various Platonic dialogues in which he appears. Thus, when Cephalus defines justice as paying ones debts, Socrates introduces the case where one returns a weapon, legally his, to a madman: it is true that this is paying a debt: but is it true that doing so is *just*?

Now one way of guaranteeing free interchange of expressions is just to *stipulate* that they will mean the same: to rule, by fiat, that a shall mean b. Then no difficulty ever will arise for none will be permitted to arise, providing only that the stipulation is accepted. Such stipulative definitions have of course their use. They are useful when we wish to have a term more convenient than the one in current use, as DNA is more convenient than dioxyriboneucleic acid. But then of course we learn nothing about the latter through having it defined as DNA: we only give ourselves licence to replace a cumbersome expression with a brisk one. Socrates, in his various investigations into the meaning of "justice" or "piety" or "knowledge" or "love" was concerned to arrive at a definition which expressed the very essence or nature of the thing defined. Such a definition would be genuinely informative: he is searching for a *real* in contrast with a *nominal* definition, an analysis of a concept rather than a handy word. A *real* definition is itself a sentence which is true or false, whereas a nominal definition ("Let *a* mean *b*!") is only a proposal, fit or unfit, but never true or false.

Suppose, now, that '*a*' is the real definition of '*b*'; then it has to be true that there is nothing to which '*a*' correctly applies and '*b*' does not, and conversely. As we have seen "applies correctly to the same [set of] things" cannot be accepted as an analysis of "has the same meaning as." First, of course, because sometimes there just may be no things to which a pair of synonymous terms applies, as with, for example, "unicorn" and "savage one-horned quadruped docile only to virgins." Moreover, a pair of terms may apply to all the same things without having the same meaning, as "largest city in the United States" applies to just the same city as does "contains the tallest building in the United States," without these expressions being definitionally equivalent. That the two expressions should be co-referential would itself depend upon quite accidental geographical fact: we would learn that the tallest building was in the largest city in a country only by examining the world, not by analyzing concepts. Because he was primarily interested in conceptual analyses, Socrates was able to use as materials for research the ordinary people of Athens. It was *their* concepts about which he was seeking to become clear; and who was to guide him except them? They might be incapable, without his guidance, to bring to self-consciousness the inner structure of the elements of their conceptual scheme: but none but they could finally say whether a proposed analysis were incorrect.

14. The intuitive distinction between finding out by examining the world and finding out by examining concepts is enshrined in a

crucial, famous distinction framed by Kant: what he termed
analytic and *synthetic* judgments. A synthetic judgment, as one
would expect, puts together things and analytical judgments take
them apart. Crudely speaking, a synthetic judgment is made true
or false by the *world* (or by our experience of it) while analytical
judgments are made true or false by *understanding* alone. It follows that Kant could not have supposed that the reference of a
term should be its meaning, for then we should always have to
look to the world to determine what our terms mean. Synthetic
judgments may be understood perfectly, and it yet remains a
question whether they are true or false. But understanding analytical propositions closes that question and, for these reasons, it
sometimes is held that analytical propositions are certain but
empty, whereas synthetic propositions are informative but in-
secure. Of course, it follows from the characterization of synthetic
propositions that they can be false. But whether this entails that
we must therefore always be uncertain, in any interesting sense,
of what is expressed in synthetic propositions, depends upon
whether we can be certain that *s* if, and only if, it is logically
impossible that *s* be false. And whether this, in turn, requires that
s must itself be such that *its* denial is self-contradictory—which
is one criterion for analyticity—is certainly debatable. If a sentence
is true it follows that it cannot be false, for its being true rules the
latter out. But it might, as an absolute fact regarding a sentence,
just as such, be that its falsehood is logically possible, even though
the sentence itself is true. These are not incompatible, one would
think; and so it seems implausible to restrict certitude to analytical
propositions alone. To say that I must be uncertain because the
sentence which expresses what I would claim to know is itself not
a *logical* certitude, is as deep-rooted a fallacy as any philosophy
affords.

Be this as it may, Kant's distinction has been the crux of intensive critical discussion concerning its viability. It has been
objected that no finally non-question-begging criterion has been
discovered for sorting sentences out or, more radically, that no such
criterion can be found in principle. In the latter event, some deep
consequences must follow. For the failure of Kant's distinction

would mean that we could not finally distinguish between discoveries made about the world and discoveries made about language. As this becomes blurred so does the distinction between the structure of our concepts and the structure of reality. Wittgenstein, in the *Tractatus* of 1922, held that there was a structural congruity between a basic language and the basic elements of the world. But this latter view is more complex: it is not that there is a matching of comparable structures, but that the structure of the world itself is so permeated with the structure of language that we cannot in principle tell the one from the other.

Apart from this profound possibility there is entailed at least a view of language itself according to which the sentences which compose it are all of a piece, hanging together in a fabric of expression, perhaps playing different roles according to their location in the fabric. In a way, to understand a sentence would then be to appreciate the way it works in the *entire system*. Attention thus is diverted from the empiricist preoccupation with the meaning of *terms*, to a new preoccupation with the meaning of *sentences*, where meaning is now conceived of as the use of a sentence in a total system of sentences which organically constitute a living language—a *language in use*. The system, or language, *serves as a whole* to articulate the experience of those who employ it and, by and large, from this perspective, we cannot so readily raise questions regarding the truth or falsity of single sentences, taken one at a time, but only for the language as a whole, which is to be held true to the extent that it serves its sole function, which is the articulation of experience and the facilitation of human existence.

At times language may break down. When it does, revision here or there will be called for. We have a range of criteria in accordance with which we may exercise the choice of what we may revise and how. The so-called analytical sentences are—or *some* of them perhaps are—deeply embedded in the language, so much so that revision of them would involve wholesale revision elsewhere in the system. The more fundamental the sentence, the more radical the conceptual revision contingent upon *its* revisions and the more radical the modification in the structure of experience itself. In the end, however, no sentence is forever immune to revision, or rejection, in view of the need for a smooth moment-to-moment functioning of the system as a whole, and with it the orderly flow of experience. This challenge to Kant's distinction, and the totalistic view of language, is due to the American philosopher W. V. Quine.

When the entire body of our propositions is connected with experience in the manner just sketched, a further distinction (and one which would seem on its face more germane to the topic of knowledge than of understanding—a distinction which itself becomes dim in view of the theory under consideration) becomes blurred. Traditionally, propositions were divided roughly along lines determined by the manner in which they could be known true. They would be *a priori* if they could be so known independently of experience, *a posteriori* if not. Knowledge of the former sort would have been naturally esteemed; it being independent of experience, experience could never prove it false. But the price for certainty was irrelevancy to experience. If experience may fluctuate madly, without its vagaries being felt within the firm shelter of *a priori* knowledge, the latter must be thoroughly independent of the former. This, to be sure, would not always have counted against it in the philosophical mind which, in one of its traditional guises, always has been disposed to hostility against experience. And moreover, does it follow from its being irrelevant to experience that *a priori* knowledge need be empty and uninformative *in toto*? It might consist of propositions, to the confirmation of which, and even to the understanding of which, experience must be irrelevant, without it following that *a priori* judgments or propositions are empty. They are so indeed if they happen, in addition to being *a priori*, to be *analytical*, having only to do with relations between the meanings of their constituent terms. But suppose instead that some of them should be synthetic?

It was Kant's thesis that there are genuinely *synthetic a priori* propositions. Since synthetic propositions *can* intelligibly be supposed false, these are informative, their truth not following from their meaning alone. But since experience is irrelevant to the determination of their truth-value, they are immune to revision in the light of untoward experience, and insofar as they are so, they enjoy a measure of certitude not commonly vouchsafed synthetic propositions. The only question is whether there is or can be *synthetic a priori* knowledge, and Kant proposed that some examples at least, though by no means not the only examples, were to be found in mathematical knowledge. If there are *some* propositions of the required sort, then plainly *synthetic a priori* knowledge is possible, and the remaining problem would be only to determine the extent and depth of such knowledge. He believed, in fact, that in metaphysics could be found further examples, but for the present let us confine ourselves just to mathematical knowledge.

15. Mathematics has always bewitched philosophers. It has since ancient times enjoyed a curiously esteemed station in the hierarchy of disciplines, though for reasons which have more to do with aesthetic considerations than crass appreciation of its applicability and utility in computational labor. Mathematics displays in its theorems and concepts a purity and rigor, an absoluteness and beauty, which the most austere abstract artist must endeavor in vain to duplicate: Euclid alone, as some poet, perhaps enviously, declared, looked on beauty bare. But in addition to these singular traits, the belief was that mathematics tells us something of the most ultimate importance regarding the deep structure of the universe. And the problem then is in what sense mathematical propositions may be counted true. Our general notion of meaning in this essay is that to know what a sentence means is to know under what conditions it will be true. But what is it that makes true " $7 + 5 = 12$," to use Kant's example? Plainly, experience does not. This does not mean, of course, that we do not certify on countless occasions that five and seven walnuts, or five and seven anythings, make twelve in all. There are ample instances and in fact no *counter*-instances. But is it merely a matter of fact that there are no counter-instances, or is it rather that we will not allow anything to be a counter-instance? Mill once proposed that if we joined pairs of objects together, to form a pair of pairs, and if, each time we did so, a fifth object spontaneously appeared, we should be obliged to say that $2 + 2 = 5$. But Mill's view has not been widely adopted. In part this is because in the case of many mathematical propositions we know to be true, it would be exceedingly difficult, and in any event arbitrary, to find instances in experience of a sort which would make counter-instances imaginable. But the general objection is that, while in the universe he imagined, the work of the world would be immeasurably facilitated —all we should need is four of any item in order thenceforward to have as many of that item as we wished—our mathematics would remain unaltered. And $2 + 2$ would be equal to 4 except where the plus-sign meant, as it does not ordinarily, the physical juxtapositions of the pairs respectively identified by the right and the left hand 2s. So it would involve at the very least a modification in mathematical notation: the equals sign would now have to be interpreted as "spontaneously produces" or some such thing; and it would then be a physical law that $2x$ juxtaposed with $2x$ physically produces $5x$. But this is not remotely like what is meant by $2 + 2 = 4$. We can *give* a physical interpretation to the operative signs, as well as to the numerical signs, but they do not have such meanings now. Mathematical sentences do not depend for their truth upon physical interpretations of their constituent elements, and, accordingly, would retain their truth-value presumably in the face of however numerically vagarious the universe should become; and while mathematics is not precisely irrelevant to the world of experience—we do, after all, count and measure—it does not appear to be made true by the latter since it cannot be made false by it.

The building into pure mathematical concepts of certain of their physical applications—it is very natural to think of addition as a physical heaping up, and subtraction as a physical 'taking away'— was inevitable, perhaps, given the origin of mathematics in the workaday contexts of accounting and land measurement; and it is only by a rigorous purgation in light of research in the foundations of mathematics that the extent of conceptual pollution could be revealed. But then as we purify our concepts of all vestiges of empirical concepts, and indemnify mathematics against the possibility of being overthrown through adverse experience, the question becomes pressing as to what, if not experience, enables us to know what it means for such propositions to be true. It is but a delaying tactic to say that they are known true because they are deducible from fundamental notions, for this merely focuses upon the status of these. Euclid, of course, regarded them as self-evident. Plato regarded them as made true by a realm of numeroid entities located in a fine, airless world outside time and space, a world of eternal forms. Appealing as this conceit must be to the poetic and mythic sensibility, it, like the view of Euclid, finds it difficult to survive the discovery of non-Euclidean geometries.

Of non-Euclidean geometries there is an infinite number. They may be generated by the systematic denial of one or another of the Euclidean postulates which, rather surprisingly, can be achieved without inconsistency. In other words, if we have a set of postulates together with p, and if p is logically independent of the set of postulates, then we can form another set, this time consisting of the same set of postulates together with the, or one of the, contraries of p. And the latter is logically consistent if the former is. We know that every non-Euclidean geometry has to be self-consistent if Euclid's geometry is. And so we have a spectacle here of an infinite number of self-consistent geometries, each mathematically impeccable, but each incompatible with the rest. So at most one of these could be true, unless there were an infinite number of Platonic realms with one geometry each. But this would make every other geometry false for a given Platonic realm, and at any rate the proliferation of Platonic realms is alien to the Platonic spirit. Again, how shall we regard a sentence as self-evident if all the versions of its denial are equally entertainable? But this not only creates difficulties for the mathematical philosophies of Plato and Euclid: it does so as well for Kant. It was, after all, Kant's thesis that mathematics, and geometry particularly, provides us knowledge, albeit *a priori*; and the possibility of infinitely many equally self-consistent but mutually incompatible geometries makes it extremely unlikely we should know which is the true one, if there even *is* a true one, on *a priori* grounds. But to appeal to experience would go counter to the alleged *a priority* and empirical irrelevance of mathematics. Nor is the problem merely restricted to geometry. For there now is the possibility of different arithmetics, "non-Cantorean" set theories, and the like. What do we do then?

When the non-Euclidean geometries were established in the

nineteenth century it seemed plausible to suppose that they had at best an imaginative relevance, for the geometry of Euclid after all appeared precisely to capture the geometrical features of the real space we lived and built our houses in. But this initial contrast could not be sustained. It was found, for example, that to insist upon the primacy, or the descriptive inviolability of Euclid's geometry entailed immense complications in physics, and, as matters developed, one could retain this geometry only at the price of complicating physical theory to the point of making it virtually unmanageable. And one could get a workable physics only by shifting to a more congenial geometry. When such a choice becomes even intelligible, it immediately becomes awkward to speak of *the* geometrical features of physical space any longer, without making some implicit reference to a body of physical theory concerned with the behavior of bodies and forces in that space. A geometry becomes spatially descriptive only when taken in conjunction with a body of *other* sorts of propositions; the entire *body* of sentences standing together in mutual support, and facing together—in rather a more complex way than the cruder empiricisms imagine—the "tribunal of experience." In view of this, we are obliged to say that geometrical propositions are synthetic. If they were analytical, by at least one rough and ready criterion of analyticity, their denial would be logically inconsistent (or inconsistent in some manner) and then *no* non-Euclidean geometry could be consistent. And they are, to a degree, *a priori*. For it may well be that no experience is in any *direct* way relevant to the ascertainment of their truth or falsity: experience may only bear directly upon some other part of the structure of geometrico-physical propositions of which they form an organic part, but bear upon the system in such a way that in order to preserve its descriptive power, changes need be made in the geometrical portions. But this will not quite vindicate Kant's thesis regarding the synthetic *a priori* status of geometrical propositions. For by the same criterion, any sentence in the system may be revised when pressure is put upon some other sector of the system, and, this being so, no basis remains for distinguishing along these lines between one portion of the system and another: every component is synthetic, and every component *a priori*: it is only that not every component can be regarded *a priori* at once in view of the fact that it is only through some contact with experience that we can speak here of truth or falsity as such.

16. Pure mathematics, then, alone remains a problem, or does so if one wishes to regard it as providing *knowledge*. It does so for *this* world only when taken in connection with mathematical impurities which are physically or psychologically presupposed in elementary operations with the counting and measuring and juxtaposing and augmentation and diminution of things. And it is far from plain that there is another world, or that things would be in any respect different when it comes to applying mathematics to it. So, when pure in the required sense, when insulated from the sorts of factors which integrate into a descriptive system portions of mathematics, it is hard to speak of mathematics as other than *a priori*, and in at least many cases, it is hard to see that they are analytical, or could be. Is it analytical that every number has a successor, or that the successor of any number is a number? Is it analytical that there are prime numbers between ten and twenty? So the question cannot really be whether mathematical sentences, in their pure state, are either *a priori* or synthetic, for they apparently can be both, but whether they provide us with knowledge. For how could they do that if there were no way of speaking of them as either true or false? One can, of course, reconstitute the notion of knowledge and truth in such a manner that the sentences of pure mathematics may be regarded merely as instruments which we may *use* in the acquisition of knowledge, but which do not, any more than test tubes, provide or express knowledge in any other way. Mathematicians may then be sophisticated instrument makers, turning out precision tools for which we may in fact never have use, and indeed to the ultimate uses of which they can themselves be indifferent. This is doubtless an acceptable account, only it is a curious one. It would be like a group of glass blowers working things out institutionally in such a way that they could blow fantastic shapes and elaborate structures, on the grounds that these might be used in some scientific work sometime, and meanwhile (they point out) their enterprise exacts a degree of aesthetic admiration, for in addition to the skill and ingenuity which goes into it, the products themselves have a delicacy, fragility, sparkle, and transparency not to be encountered elsewhere. But its curiosity need not count against it.

Or again: mathematics can be counted, as some do count it, a game of a very difficult and exacting sort, on the order of chess but rather more complex, where one builds up certain structures in conformity with rules one imposes upon oneself, it being, after all, the mark of a game that those who play it accept certain rules for the sole purposes of playing the game: one can knock an opposing queen off the board, and weaken the opposing position in so doing, but it breaks a rule, or at least does not conform to one, and if one does not keep the rules, there is no game. In this way indeed, mathematics is *a priori* and it is so only because congruity with the rules is the sole basis for deciding whether or not a move is justified. But again, this is to render experience merely irrelevant, as it is with chess.

One then may ask in what sense mathematics provides knowledge, given that it is *a priori*: and the answer must be: it gives none. So Kant would, on this account, have been right in his characterization but wrong only in thinking he was characterizing a branch of *knowledge*. Of course one can *define* "true" in terms of congruity with rules, and one can speak, if one wishes to, of knowledge by saying that one knows that *s* when *s* is shown to be congruent with a rule one has accepted, or when *s* has been reached through a series of steps executed in conformity with a set of rules one has accepted. There is no reason *not* to define truth and knowledge in these terms, and, if one does so, one will then be able to say what it means to understand a mathematical sentence: one understands it when one can say what rule it conforms to, or what set of rules permit one to reach it in a set number of steps. But this would certainly be knowledge—and truth—of a different sort than we would invoke when we claimed to know that a certain sentence about the world is true. So it would not be as though Kant had marked off two species within the genre of knowledge, viz., knowledge *a priori* and knowledge *a posteriori*: rather there would be two quite distinct genres of knowledge, distinct in the sense that radically different criteria would be applicable for ascertaining what it meant to know something. In mathematics, knowledge would be relativized to a set of rules one happened to adopt: within a set of rules there would be no room for maneuver, but a choice always would be possible *between* sets of rules. And this returns us to our discussion of alternative geometries. Within a given geometry one has little license, or none, for the choices one makes. But one can choose between alternative systems. And one's criterion of choosing then would be not a mathematical nor a *geometrical* choice (these being *internal* choices) but some other; the criterion then might be the general one of congruity with experience, or facilitation of science, or some such thing. But in that case we will have reverted to a sense of knowledge and of truth which is of a piece with our understanding of these concepts in their application to statements regarding the world. But since these are matters sufficiently distinct from those which have to do with meaning and understanding, which have guided us thus far, we might fittingly turn now to the second set of philosophical problems we roughly marked off in Section 6—the problems, by and large, of knowledge.

III ← KNOWLEDGE

17. If to understand a sentence *s* is to know under what conditions *s* would be true, then to *know* that *s* is true must be to know these conditions to be satisfied. And here we must examine that treacherous passage which crosses the gap between the vehicles of meaning, and that which vests them with semantical values. That this passage is considered treacherous by philosophers is borne witness to by the possibility of skeptical obstacles at every hand, obstacles so strangely complicated that the philosophers who have served as cartographers of this gap have often despaired of ever crossing it safely. The possibility of safe passage has been the abiding preoccupation of philosophy at least since Descartes, who raised the question in its most radical form, namely, whether *anything* was immune to doubt? And what if nothing was?

Descartes argued more or less as follows. Consider the grounds I have, or would spontaneously describe myself as having, for believing any of the class of sentences of which a given sentence is a member. Thus I believe there is a pigeon on my sill. I would claim to know this on the grounds that I see and hear it there. And these grounds are typical for a very large class of sentences indeed: if I know or claim to know them, this will be because of something which can be referred to such senses as seeing and hearing. But the senses can, in fact, deceive me; and if the senses are, or even *can* be, defective in providing me with grounds for believing what I do, and if the only basis I have for grounded belief here is that I sense something, for all I can know on *this* basis, what I believe is false. Thus my sense experience might be just as it is, and there be no pigeon on the sill. In general, if the sole grounds to which we can intelligibly appeal for justifying a given belief will not guarantee us against that belief being false, we have no basis for knowing it to be true. This being so, all such propositions as I am disposed to believe on those grounds must be held in abeyance. Accordingly we require grounds for beliefs which *do* guarantee what we would pretend to know on the basis of such grounds; and if there are no such grounds, whatever we are disposed to believe could be false, and we can pretend to no genuine knowledge whatever: the entire body of propositions which passes at a given time for the sum of human knowledge must be placed within the brackets of skeptical suspension of belief. The search for belief-guaranteeing grounds constitutes, then, the theory of knowledge.

Descartes's strategy is instructive. A class of propositions is defined relative to the grounds we have for justifiably claiming to know them. The grounds for a given such class fails *in principle* to guarantee that members of that class are true or false when conditions can be imagined under which the grounds hold and the conditions fail. So, unless no such condition can be imagined, the grounds will always be inadequate for the propositions they define, and the latter must be inacceptable as expressions of genuine knowledge. They may be true. But then, consistent with all the same grounds, they may be false. And if the grounds may be the same while the propositions vary in truth value, how shall we pretend to truth when those are the only grounds which justify the pretense? Upon succeeding in imagining a "ground for doubt," then, Descartes seeks for another class of propositions specifically immune to it and defined by a different set of grounds altogether. This procedure goes on until grounds impervious to doubt are found which define a class of propositions secure, henceforth, from his corrosive methods, or until we reconcile ourselves to knowing nothing with certainty. Let us illustrate this descent.

18. Consider, once more, propositions based upon the senses. To be sure, the senses deceive me. How do I know this? Surely, I know this in part through the senses. Do I not, for example, discover through closer looks that my eyes have deceived me in a given case? That what I took to be a pigeon was a bit of paper? True. But if I am to reject all propositions based upon the senses because the senses are defective, I must apparently also reject the proposition that the senses are defective—and hence cut the ground out from under my rejection of these grounds. Either that, it seems, or the senses provide, along with their defects, a simultaneous remedy. The objection that the senses deceive then collapses into silliness or self-stultification. Descartes meets this sort of cleverness with brilliance. I could be certain, under optimal conditions, that my senses were not deceiving me—having taken the paradigmatic "closer look" under ideal conditions of illumination and the like—providing only I were *certain that I were sensing*. But I might not be. I might, for example, just be dreaming that I am sensing something under optimal perceptual conditions. And how could the senses help me here, when I am not even sure that I am sensing?

Philosophers have found this argument almost paralyzingly compelling. But Descartes pressed on past the objection, seeking for sentences against which it would be impotent, e.g., sentences such that the grounds for claiming to know them do not presuppose either that I am awake or sensing. And perhaps with mathematics, to the truth or falsity of which (as we saw) it is at least plausible to suppose that sense experience is altogether irrelevant, with mathematics I might have attained a haven of certitude. As it happened, Descartes did not pause even here. A malign demon, he proposed, might undetectingly be working a distortion upon his mind, so that whenever he proposed a sentence *he* could imagine no ground for doubting, he nevertheless would be wrong in supposing it immune to doubt. Here it is not a matter of his imagining grounds for doubt, but rather *imagining* that they can be imagined; and unless this can be voided, nothing remains certain after all, and knowledge remains logically beyond his grasp. Surely, it must seem, that if we must find propositions against which we cannot imagine that grounds for doubt can be imagined, we can find no certain propositions whatever.

Descartes triumphed over the malign demon with an argument

I must paraphrase as follows. In order to be mistaken, I must affirm some proposition, must actually think some proposition to be true. Now though each proposition *I* think true *may* be false, I must *think them to be true* or I cannot be mistaken. So, if I am mistaken at all, I must think something true, and if I am always mistaken, I am always thinking some proposition or other true. About that there can be no mistake, since it is logically presupposed by the very meaning of the concept of *mistakeness*. So let the demon wreak his worst, he cannot make it be that I am always mistaken: for if I were I would know at least that I were thinking, and since I could not be mistaken about that, the hypothesis that I always am mistaken is self-defeating. Having established this, Descartes then gathered together the presuppositions of its establishment to establish that he himself existed, since, for him to be mistaken, *he* had to venture propositions, and so exist. And, since he could not think of himself as not thinking—the very act of doing so required him to be thinking, and so again, the thought of himself as not thinking appeared, by courtesy of a near pun, to be self-destructive—he concluded that he was logically a thinking thing. It is a curiosity of his philosophy that it almost cannot be generated except on what appears the most damaging of all hypotheses, viz., that he always is mistaken, but it is not convenient at this point to examine his proofs of his own existence and nature. Rather, given that he exists and is what he thinks he is, can he have grounds for believing that there is anything *other* than himself? Descartes thought there were; he thought, indeed, that he could demonstrate the existence of God! And in the present context, it will be quite useful to pay some attention to the notion of existence. This shunts us back to considerations in the topic of meaning, but in weaving the fabric of philosophy, we cannot avoid that sort of shuttling back and forth.

19. In medieval philosophy a distinction was drawn between *essence* and existence. Let us roughly state what the essence of something would be. The essence of an object *o* would be described with a set of terms *T*, such that *T* defines what it is to be an *o*: whatever is *T* is an *o*, and nothing not *T* can be *o*. Thus the essence of the *o*'s would be the set of *o*-defining traits, and to understand what "*o*" means is to have mastered a *real definition* (to use a notion already introduced): if "*T*" is the real definition of "*o*," then *T* describes the essence of the *o*'s. It was the Aristotelian, as it was the Socratic view, that to achieve understanding of something was one with determining the real definition of that thing, and, in medieval terms, this became one with discovering essences. To know what man essentially is, is to know what "man" really means. Now the medievals held, correctly, that it is not ordinarily part of the definition, or essence of something, that *there are* things *of which* the definition should be true. One always can meaningfully ask, having mastered the definition of *o*'s, whether there are in fact any *o*'s, or, whether *o*'s *exist*. It is not part of the meaning of "triangle," to take a stock example, that there are triangles, or that triangles exist. And from this it generally follows that the meaning of a term is invariant as to whether or not there are things to which it applies. Hence it is never meaningless, though perhaps sometimes false, to deny the existence of triangles, or cats, or anything whatever. So existence is not, in general, a defining property of anything, or better, it is not a property to all. So to say that a triangle exists is only to say that the essence of triangles is exemplified in some object. And this is not to say something about triangles really at all: it is, rather, to say something about the concept or essence of the term. To put the matter then into medieval terms, *existence* is not entailed by essence, which means that understanding does not entail knowledge; we can understand all that we do understand without knowing whether anything exists at all. "Exists" then plays a role in connection with terms comparable, semantically, to the role played by "true" in connection with sentences. It is against the background of the essence-existence distinction that we must appreciate a great many philosophical theories. Thus, certainly, one central claim of empiricism may now be stated as this: certain terms cannot be understood unless there are instances to which they apply, for I could not understand simple terms unless I in fact experienced instances of them; so, for at least some terms, understanding, though it does not logically entail knowledge, nevertheless cannot be had unless knowledge is had as well. And again, against the medieval claim that essences do not logically depend upon existence, we must appreciate the recent, bold, but essentially medieval, theory of Jean-Paul Sartre, that man has an existence but not an essence: that in contrast with those essences which do not logically require instances, man is an instance without an essence, whose career consists in self-definition: man is not so much what he *becomes* as he is the (logically foredoomed) process of becoming it. But these are matters not to be chased down here.

Now there are immense problems with the notion of essences, some of them metaphysical; for example: *are* there essences, as special sorts of entities in the world, and do we want to suppose they are anything other than just ways of thinking? (This is very like the problem of Section 12 concerning meanings.) And again, there are difficulties with essential definitions, difficulties seized upon, amongst others, by Wittgenstein, who demanded whether there *must* be any one set of conditions necessary and sufficient for something to be an *o*; what, he asked, is the essence of being a *game*? And he went on to imply that, if there is an essence of games here (which is doubtful) it is plain that we would have to look hard to find it; and *we* certainly do not know that something is a game on the basis of knowing that it instantiates some "real definition" of gamehood!

But the distinction between essence and existence does not especially depend upon any resolution of these questions: all that we must do, in order to utilize it, is to appreciate the difference between understanding a term and knowing whether there is anything to which that term correctly applies. And it is plain that there are many terms we understand, and hence concepts we have mastered, whether or not there are instances for these concepts and where, more important, it is not logically requisite that, in order for there to be the understanding there is, there in fact have to *be* instances. So understanding, in this quite special sense, is neither augmented by the existence, nor diminished by the non-existence of instances. We should, of course, immensely augment our understanding of unicorns if unicorns there were. But our understanding of the *concept* of unicorn would not be extended:

we would be finding out interesting facts about unicorns, but nothing new or interesting with regard to the meaning of "unicorn."

To this there was apparently to be one exception. In the tradition in which Descartes was working, there was a famous argument to the effect that at least, but also at most in the *one case* of God, existence *is* of the very essence. And now we must say something about the Ontological Argument, invented by the great thinker Anselm of Canterbury, which exploits this notion. Anselm's argument is intricately ramified in its presuppositions, and perhaps not even now, after several centuries of debate, does one know how to deal with the issues, or what precisely are the issues, which it raises. Crudely, the argument runs as follows. We must have some idea of God, even if we deny that God exists, for unless we have some such idea, it is difficult to see what we could suppose ourselves intelligibly to be denying. And unless our idea of God is the idea of a being than whom a greater cannot be conceived, we have not a correct idea of God at all. For if something greater than God were conceivable, *that* would be God, and what we thought was God could not have been Him. Logically speaking, nothing greater than God is conceivable. Now, Anselm argues, God must exist. For if He does not, it is after all possible to conceive of a being greater than God, namely, a being in every respect like the God of whom we conceived, except that *this* one exists: for it is greater to exist than not to. (A God which could not exist would be impotent to exist, and it would be easy to conceive of a God greater than that!) But now, we have succeeded in conceiving of a being greater than God. But that is impossible, by hypothesis. So God (logically) has to exist, since it is demonstrably self-contradictory to affirm that the being than whom a greater is inconceivable does not exist.

Anselm's argument was capped by a clever monk of his time, Gaunilon. He proposed, by perfectly analogous argumentation, to establish the existence of the greatest island conceivable and, working along such lines, we can establish, apparently, the existence of whatever it is than which a greater is inconceivable. This is not altogether legitimate, I think: for though we may conceive of an island than which a greater *island* cannot be conceived, God must certainly be greater than any island than which a greater is inconceivable, for God is the greatest *being* logically conceivable: and Anselm's argument only works for the greatest conceivable being. But Anselm fell back upon *this* notion: that a man could not honestly be said to have understood "God"—or the concept of God —if he supposes it possible that God does not exist. A man who pretends to understand what triangles are, and then wonders whether there could be two-sided triangles, is misguided in his first pretension: he has not understood at all. And so if someone wonders whether God exists, he cannot both entertain that wonder and pretend to have understood: in God's case, His essence is His existence.

But it is not plain that this latter strategy is available. For after all, the uses of "essence" and "existence" were always taught in logical contrast with one another. To say that, in this one instance, they do *not* contrast, verges upon nonsense: it would be like proposing that, in the case of God, His left side *is* His right side. Or, perhaps, the issue might be more philosophically put this way. Suppose existence *is*, in some sense, part of the essence of God. Then, surely, the question arises whether, in the *old* sense of "exists," God exists; which is to ask: is this new concept instantiated? And we should still be able, logically, to entertain the question whether God exists. And all we would have done would have been to introduce a novel sense of "exists" which is useless for the purposes it would have been introduced to serve.

This line of criticism is very largely due to Kant, who pointed out that "exists" is not a real predicate, that it is not real in the sense that one is saying nothing about a thing when one says that it exists, that "exists" says only something about concepts, and about them says that they are instantiated. As Russell was to say later, it is nonsense to say that things exist, and equally nonsense to say that they do not. It is nonsense in the way in which it is nonsense to say that chairs are even or that chairs are odd, oddness and evenness being predicable only of things of a different type altogether than chairs exemplify. But even with concepts, to say that "exists" applies to them is not to say something of the sort said with "Concepts are clear" or "Concepts are useful." Existence is not a property, not certainly a mysterious property, of things; and it is not a property, either, of concepts. It is, if anything, a value which is attached to concepts only when concepts have instances.

20. It may be seen from these considerations how immensely attractive ontological arguments must have appeared to Descartes. For it is not plain that he really allowed himself room for answering the question whether anything other than himself existed, unless ontological argumentation would permit an affirmative answer. It is philosophically altogether instructive to see in what manner Descartes put himself in such a position that recourse to ontological argument was so desperately required. And we must ask what would be the consequences for him—or for anyone if his arguments were sound—if ontological arguments should be, as we have contended that they are, inherently fallacious. The consequence, of course, is that we should have no certitude that, other than ourselves, there is anything: no world, no persons, nothing. Such a dismal position is called *solipsism*, and though, of course, none of us especially would wish to be a solipsist, the question is essentially how to avoid being forced into being one. The problem is not so much to *prove* that there is anything other than oneself, but rather, to see how one might inadvertently find oneself committed to the view that no such proof is possible. Let us then examine the sort of circumstances which lead to this. Once more, let us begin with some questions of perception.

Whether I in fact see a distant tower, or only seem to see one, the fact remains that my *experience* at the moment is exactly what it is whichever of these alternatives hold. Hence there seems to be something, some core of experience, which is invariant as to the two cases. But exactly the same considerations arise when, with Descartes, we suppose there is no way of telling from anything internal to our experience, whether we see anything at all or are only *seeming* to be seeing, which would be the case in a dream. Once more, there would seem to be some invariant core of experience common to the two cases. And similar considerations apply in some cases of illusion and in all cases of delusion or hallucination. Now since there are these cases where, whether or not there is something "there," I in fact have an experience, I in fact experience *something*; and since whatever it is I experience in these cases is *invariant* and indiscernible with regard to the differences between the two sorts of cases, it is at least plausible to suppose that it is *this* invariant core which is the object of my experience—whatever further differences there may be to the two cases. Nothing *internal* to my experience tells me, thus, that I am seeing or only seeming to see. So the differences, however they are to be accounted for, must be external to experience, and we can describe our experience regardless of whether we are sustaining illusion or not: the content of experience itself seems neutral with respect to this difference.

The neutralization of the content of experience makes this content function, in epistemological discussions, very much in the manner in which sentences—or meaning-vehicles—functioned in our earlier discussions. There, recall, we proposed that one may understand a meaning-vehicle independently of what particular semantical value it might bear, if it bears any semantical value at all. Here the content of experience may be understood whether it is "veridical" or "non-veridical"—which is in effect to attach semantical values to one's experience. And very naturally, as with meaning-vehicles generally, it must appear that the semantical values of these new meaning-vehicles must be externally conferred. And this is almost a paraphrase of the observation that nothing internal to the content of a given experience will differentiate it as veridical or not: if there were some internal criterion, the problem of differentiating dreams from the experiences of waking life would be of a piece exactly with differentiating blue from red.

When we take these somewhat abstract considerations in conjunction with a curious fact of nomenclature, we derive some curious consequences. This fact is that the content of experience, or the objects of experience, were invariably called "ideas" by those philosophers of the seventeenth and eighteenth centuries whose collective efforts virtually created the theory of knowledge as understood in modern times. When I thus would describe myself as seeing a dog, these philosophers would describe me as having an *idea*, the idea of a dog. And since the difference between this dog-idea being genuine or illusory must be determined by some factor external to the idea as such, the answer to what these external factors are, and how they confer the value upon ideas which I cannot infer from the idea itself, will be an answer to a question in what we must term the *theory of experience*, or the *theory of perception*. And it is an interesting fact that the content of experience, or perception, is a datum which is taken for granted by theorists of perceptions: all of their differences have to do with these external questions.

21. One natural answer to the question of when does my idea bear the positive semantical value is this: it does so when it is caused by and resembles something "of which" it is the idea: the idea of a dog, thus, is veridical, when it is caused by a dog and resembles the dog which causes it. It bears the negative semantical value when it fails to resemble its cause. This theory, which is in fact not terribly remote from what one might regard as almost a scientific account based upon the physiology of perception, is often called the representationalist theory, viz., that an idea "represents" its cause, and is often attributed, not as its originator but as its most notable exponent, to John Locke. Attractive as representationalism is, it raises some immense problems, chief amongst which is how we should know either that it is true or how, in any given case, we ever should know whether our idea in fact bears the positive or negative semantical value. The first is more vexing as a problem if we subscribe, as Locke did, to the view that whatever we know derives in some fashion from experience, for in that case our incapacity to know in any single case the value of our ideas logically undercuts the possibility of our knowing representationalism to be true. So let us concentrate merely upon the latter problem. Locke answered, simply, that we know that our idea is veridical by comparing it with its original. This is modeled on the notion of comparing portraits with their subjects, with, unfortunately, this difference: the very possibility of the comparison is ruled out by the theory itself. For how are we to achieve experience of the "original" in order to achieve the comparison? Any experience we may hope to have of it will be only another idea: so the hope of comparing originals with ideas leaves us rather comparing ideas with other ideas, and the entire ambition of getting outside, or behind, the screen of ideas into which we have enclosed ourselves is logically foredoomed.

That we only can compare other ideas with a given idea was first pointed out as a consequence of representationalism by George Berkeley, who rather cheerfully endorsed it. To be sure, it is bad news for the representationalist. He not only has no way of knowing whether his ideas are in any instance true or false: he has no way of knowing whether his entire theory is true or false, or even of explaining how he could have hit upon such a theory. And, no less important, he could not any longer be sure there was anything external to his ideas, each of which, for all he now could know, could be illusory! And this is precisely the state of affairs in which Descartes found himself when he resorted to the desperate measure of ontological argumentation. Descartes argued roughly thus: I have an overwhelming belief that my ideas are caused, that they are in many cases caused by something other than myself, and that they resemble their causes in at least some of those cases. But I have, unfortunately, no non-circular way of demonstrating this belief to be true in all, or even any of its elements, unless there should be *some* idea which bears on its face, so to speak, its causal origins. The idea of God alone appeared to him to be logically capable of this, and indeed it would be (on grounds of the ontological argument) logically impossible that it should be an idea of God and *not* resemble that of which it was an idea. And in a truly ingenious way, Descartes went on to contend that my having the idea of God can only be explained by invoking a cause at least as powerful as I conceive of God to *be*—and this is just to say that I could not have the idea of God unless it were in fact caused by God; for what cause could be as powerful as I conceive of God to be which was not God Himself—since I conceive of God as a being than whom a greater is inconceivable? So Descartes comfortably concluded that he was not alone in the universe. But if ontological argumentation fails in principle, as we have proposed it does, then Descartes has no exit from the world of (mere) ideas. And neither does any of us if the representationalist is right. We are left with a class of absolutely irresoluble doubts concerning the existence, no less than the nature, of the "external world," so-called.

22. A quite strikingly brilliant dissolution of these problems is due to Berkeley, who ironically suggested that our complaints are due to a dust we ourselves have raised, and that once we realize this, doubts of the sort which appear to blind us will be forever laid to rest. His theory, in its simplest form, is this: there is no difference between the external world and our ideas for there to be a discrepancy between them. Instead of supposing that the ideas I have are caused by something other than themselves, which are the *real* objects of experience, why not suppose that the real objects of experience just are the ideas themselves? The world is not *represented* by our ideas, the world just *is* our ideas. This theory sounds immensely implausible to begin with, so cracked indeed, and so fertile in generating perplexities of its own, that one may wonder in fact whether it is to be preferred to the sensible dilemmas of the representationalist theory. The latter at least permits us to sustain, without justifying, the belief that other than our own ideas there is something, whatever may be its nature. But Berkeley's system permits no such thing. If the world just is my ideas, there can apparently be nothing to the world other than my ideas. It is not just that the only thing I can suppose to exist with any assurance is what I happen at a moment to be experiencing: rather, the ideas I have at a given time are the only things it apparently now *makes sense* to say exist at all! For what is an idea? It is what I experience at a given moment. So the only ideas there are are those I experience at a given moment. And if the world just is my ideas, the world must exist just at a given moment, and consist solely of the ideas I have at that moment. It was Berkeley's thesis that to be *is* to be perceived (*esse est percipi*) — on which principle he hoped to show that the world just *is* our perceptions.

But the consequence just noted is deeply offensive to common sense: for it is our belief, a belief at least as entrenched as the one

Descartes invoked, that the world goes on existing between our perceptions of it, and that there is more to it than what I perceive at any given moment. And we believe that the world existed long before, and will, unhappily, exist long after we ourselves no longer exist. We cannot take it with us. How is Berkeley to resolve this? It is a curious fact that at just this crucial point, he, like Descartes, invokes God. The world has, he maintains, just the stability we suppose and just the nature he proposed: it is perceived by God, and, as the idea of God, or made as it is entirely of the ideas which God has, it exists eternally, and exists, moreover, between and external to *our* perceptions. This is a startling metaphysical consequence which Berkeley, who was a bishop, was thoroughly delighted to draw. That the existence of God should be logically presupposed in order to support our most deeply embedded beliefs of common sense was almost as good as an ontological proof! To be sure, we must conclude that in a curious sense, the world is mental in whatever way our ideas are mental, which sounds more startling than it need, given the antecedent unclarity with which we understand this notion of mentality anyway. But at least we have no longer any need to invoke things hidden behind our experience. God is the only explanatory notion we require.

Philosophers since Berkeley, who have been impressed with the rigor of his empiricism, have balked at paying the theological price Berkeley was happy to pay (and would have been unhappy not to pay had he thought one could get by without it) for sustaining it. They have reconstructed Berkeley roughly along these lines. To say that an object *o* exists although I am not experiencing *o*, means only that if I *were* in the right place at the right time and under the proper circumstances, I *would* have certain *o*-experiences. Then, if to perceive *o* is *in fact* to have certain *o*-experiences, the theory here advanced will preserve Berkeley's program of analyzing things totally into experiential terms, without having to take on the theological commitment which, though it was perhaps Berkeley's main philosophical motive, has seemed to many incompatible with the thoroughgoing empiricism of the remainder of his system. The theory that all sentences about physical objects are analyzable into statements about experience which either we do have or which we would have under propitious circumstances, is known as *phe-nomenalism*. Phenomenalism, it must be stressed, is not merely, or perhaps not even, a theory of knowledge, so much as it is a theory of understanding and a theory of being. And concerning this a few words must be said. It is a theory of understanding, whose claim is that every meaningful unit of discourse is definable without remainder into a set of terms, each of which must have reference to sense-experience. As a theory of meaning, it is, of course, subject to some refined and difficult objections, to the overcoming of which phenomenalists have devoted extraordinary ingenuity. But that it should raise further questions is not to be held against it; and, in its own terms at least, it can claim to have solved Berkeley's problem, to have salved common sense, and to have provided a theory of meaningfulness which alone seems consonant with the fundamental teachings of empiricism. It claims, finally, to answer how we know whether anything other than ourselves exists. To exist is to be perceived or (if we are to remain within the domain of discourse which phenomenalism licenses as meaningful) to be *in principle* perceivable. So it is ingenuous to wonder, having experienced something, whether what we experience exists. There lingers a question, however, of whether "*o* exists unperceived" can really be said to mean that we would, under the proper circumstances, have *o*-experiences. But the phenomenalist might reply that if it does mean more than that, we might at least *say* what more it means. And to this challenge it is not altogether easy to rise.

There are, however, some things we can say. First, let us grant, in order to concentrate upon the essential issues, the phenomenalist's claim that in principle every term ostensibly used to describe a physical object may be translated exactly and perfectly into some set of terms which have reference to sense experience alone. There may be obstacles to the achievement of this, but let us for the present merely disregard them. Let [e] then be the actual phenomenalistic translation of *o*. Now replace *o* with [e] in the expression "*o* exists unperceived," and in the expression "*o* would be perceived if . . ." where the blank is itself to be filled in with whatever perceptual conditions the phenomenalist requires for his analysis. It may be observed at this point that there is at least a difference in grammatical mood between these two sentences: the first is in the indicative and the second in the subjunctive moods.

Mere difference of mood may not count for a great deal, but it may be pointed out that some serious philosophers have rested upon no weightier a distinction some extraordinarily momentous philosophical theories. It has, thus, been argued that ethical sentences really are covert *imperatives*, that the seeming indicative "*o* is good" is in effect the covert imperative "Approve of *ȯ*!" And since not itself an indicative, and since imperatives cannot be logically deduced from indicatives, the conclusion appears unmistakable that no number, however large, of indicative sentences will logically entail an imperative. We cannot, as the slogan runs, derive an "ought" from an "is"; and hence our moral propositions are logically independent of our factual knowledge. Well, it is not plain that the logical distance between indicatives and subjunctives is any narrower than that between indicatives and imperatives. But let us work this out in some detail.

Suppose that I in fact perceive *o*, and am under conditions *c*. Then is it not true that *o would be* perceived under these conditions? If it is, then "*o* would be perceived under *c*" is compatible both with "*o* is perceived under *c*" and "*o* is not perceived under *c*" —and *these* ordinarily are incompatible with one another. So, if "*o* would be perceived under *c*" is a *translation* of the latter, it should be incompatible with the former. For if *s* and *s'* are incompatible, and *t* is a translation of *s*, *s'* and *t* would have to be incompatible. But there is another problem. Suppose we were to specify the conditions under which *o* is perceived. Is it not ordinarily supposed that at least one of these conditions is that *o* exist? For how can what does not exist be perceived? If this is so, then to specify the condition *c* under which *o* would be perceived requires that we list that *o* exists. Then "*o* would be perceived under *c*" would not be a translation of "*o* exists" (unperceived) for the notion of existence is already built into the conditions *c* and the definition is circular. To give up this as one of the conditions is to weaken the equation of existence with perceivability. What clearly emerges from this is that the phenomenalist hopes to translate the very concept of *existence* into phenomenalistic terms. And this goes well beyond [e]! For [e] gave us the whole meaningful content of '*o*.' But—as our brush with scholasticism should have taught us—existence is never part of the meaning of a concept. So if "exists" is not a predicate, it is not a *phenomenal* predicate either. If phenomenalism stands or falls on the basis of whether it can give a phenomenalistic rendering of existence, there is strong reason to suspect it falls, even granting what we have in this paragraph. As we should suspect, existence is not somehow quite the sort of notion we can suppose capable of phenomenalist translation. And this will be strengthened in the sequel.

23. It cannot honestly be said that the belief that our ideas are caused by external objects which they resemble (which Descartes found overwhelming) is the plain man's belief or even a belief of common sense, inasmuch as the plain man is not ordinarily a representationalist. Nor is the plain man likely to be a Berkeleyan phenomenalist, in part because some distinction will be drawn by him between things and ideas of things, and he would suppose that when he perceives a rock it is actually that stony lump (and not an idea of a rock) which is the object of his perception. Such a view is called naïve realism. And the reason that the realist will not countenance an identification of rocks with ideas is that he believes rocks exist unperceived, while ideas could not. And he does not suppose that all he means by saying that they exist unperceived is that someone would have certain experiences were he to be under certain conditions. So the realist must equally oppose phenomenalism. Plainly, we cannot have actual experiences of things existing unperceived; the realist must be making an assumption which a thoroughgoing empiricist would find adventurous at best and meaningless at worst. It must be plain that the assumption of the continuity of objects, such as rocks, in the intervals between anyone's perceptions of them, is a theory introduced (perhaps unconsciously) in order to assure a degree of stability in our world which, otherwise, would be radically threatened were objects to disappear when unperceived. The *content* of experience is the same, whichever theory of experience we may subscribe to,

whether we are phenomenalists or representationalists or realists. So these competing theories could hardly be discriminated between on the grounds of experience itself. These theories are not so much different theories of experience as they are differing metaphysics: for rocks would have radically different properties, obviously, if they were physical objects than if they were ideas. So that disagreement is plainly over the ultimate constitution of the objects of experience. If this is true, then phenomenalism must appear metaphysically neutral as between these views.

But something stronger than this can be said in favor of phenomenalism as we add to it a theory of meaningfulness which empiricism is natively predisposed to affirm: that a term is meaningful only insofar as either it is an experiential term, or explicitly definable in some set of such terms. And if this is defensible, then, since obviously what divides the Berkeleyan from the realist, and both from the representationalist, cannot pass muster, the differences between their theories must be referred to factors *inherently external* to experience. And if no experience can be relevant to discriminating amongst them, they are demonstrably metaphysical theories, collapsing into emptiness and nonsense. This leaves the phenomenalist the victory almost by default—only providing that the phenomenalist correctly captures the notion of unperceived existence. Obviously, if our argument has been correct, phenomenalists cannot get an experiential translation of the notion of existence, existence not being a property of objects anyway. But it must seem as though this almost takes care of the remaining problem. For it is not a defect in phenomenalism that it cannot achieve translation of a term which has no experiential equivalent, as "exists" has not. But then phenomenalism, like its rivals, must make use of at least *one* notion, namely existence, which would have to be rejected as meaningless by purely empiricist criteria. If it admits this, then it cannot any longer reject its rivals on these grounds. Well, it might say, let the concept of existence be ruled out as meaningless as well! That is a heroic strategy, but it will unfortunately dissolve phenomenalism as a theory of experience, as a philosophical theory. So the heroic move is a Kamikaze heroism, culminating in suicide. Let us expatiate on this.

Both idealism, of Berkeley's sort, and naïve realism are attempts to obviate the need for ideas which serve as intermediaries between ourselves and the world. But since these intermediating, representational entities were introduced in response to the problem of illusion, we are now obliged to say that unless either of these rival positions is able to come up with an acceptable alternative solution (not equally embarrassing in its consequences and not equally vulnerable in terms of its own criteria, as is representationalism), they cannot be preferred to it. After all, philosophical theories arise in response to problems; and rival theories must at the least be able to solve the same problems.

Let us once again recall that nothing internal to an experience will differentiate it as illusory or non-illusory, genuine or hallucinatory. It is this which was seized upon by representationalism, which, seeing that the differences had to be external to an experience, took this external determination to be a question of whether or not a relationship of representation was sustained between the experience and what it was caused by. And as we saw, it is a chief difficulty of this view that we really have no way of finding out if the relationship required does hold. So while representationalism has a theory of the external differences between genuine and non-genuine experiences, it unfortunately allows no manner of applying that theory, and quite abruptly leads into a skeptical impasse: the external factors which make the required difference now constitute the *external world*, as it is called; and the representationalist has no way of telling, from the experiences he has, how or whether the external world *is*. It is against these factors that we must appreciate the strategies of the rivals of representationalism. For neither phenomenalism nor realism can possibly have recourse to "external" correspondences between experience and the world (both phenomenalism and realism hold that we *experience* the world, differing only in their views of what sort of world we experience), and both have to give *some* account of illusory experience.

The typical move made here by phenomenalism is to invoke a criterion of *coherency of experience*. An experience is illusory if it fails to cohere with a body of experiences regarded as non-illusory or "genuine." Now before analyzing this notion, it must in fairness be remarked that it is not an inaccurate representation of how ordinarily we *do*, in common life, proceed. One sees a dagger, like Macbeth did, and reaching for its handle, one's fist closes upon nothingness. Because one has a right to expect, on the basis of past experience, the experience of solidity which comes with the grasping of dagger hafts, and because this expectation is in the present instance mysteriously frustrated, one classifies the visual experience, which provoked the attempted grasping, as having been illusory. It failed to cohere with a body of largely self-coherent past experience.

There are, of course, serious objections to coherency as a criterion of reality. Suppose thus that a pair of experiences should be mutually incoherent. How shall we distinguish the illusory from the non-illusory one? Is this not a purely arbitrary choice? Given that p and *not-p* are contradictory, we know that they cannot both be coherently asserted. But knowing that both cannot be does not tell us which of the two *can* be. Well, in a sense this is a justified objection. But the phenomenalist will say that one only can go on, amass a body of experience, and then decide to assert whatever is coherent with the mass, rejecting as illusory whatever the mass logically rejects. And do we not, in fact, function just this way, integrating our experiences together into a cohering mass? And if mere *incoherence* impresses you as insufficient to relegate a given experience to the status of an illusion, the phenomenalist doubtless will reply that we still are probably dominated by either representationalist prejudices, or else by some lingering hope that illusory experiences are intrinsically marked—and in the latter case there would be no problem and in the former case there would be no solution. *His* account, he may continue, rather neatly solves the problem and does so in a way which is continuous with common practice.

24. There can be little doubt that illusory experiences are inconsistent with the mass of experiences taken as veridical. The only question is whether this is what "illusory experience" *means*. And once more, it must be remembered, the phenomenalist, in insisting upon the latter point, is undertaking to salvage—in a way

we must by now recognize as ruthlessly empirical—a concept thought to be external to experience and hence, by phenomenalist criteria, meaningless: he has attempted to give some empirical meaning to the notion of genuineness and illusoriness as a distinction *within* experience, rather than as something which is a function of some relationship between experience and the *world*. And if we balk at accepting his recommendations, he might, as phenomenalists typically do, ask us what further than incoherence with a reference class of self-coherent experiences one can mean by "illusory experience." It is this challenge which realism must meet.

A realist may contend that we must at least distinguish between illusory experiences and, as we may call it, experiences of illusions. By an experience of an illusion, I mean, for example, being shown an illusion by a psychologist, perhaps one of the optical illusions one finds in psychology textbooks. Illusions, in the latter sense, are amongst the things which the world contains. I can point to one of them and say: there is an illusion. An illusion is what it *is*, just as rocks are rocks and trees are trees. Again, we must learn to distinguish trees from their reflections in water or in reflecting surfaces generally. But it is a fact about the world that there are in it reflections of things as well as the things themselves. One may mistake the mirror-image of a cat for a cat, and throwing a shoe at it, break the mirror. But so might one mistake a cat for a mirror-image of a cat, and, thinking it is a mirror image, refrain from throwing the shoe. There just are illusions in the world which it would be a *mis*take to take for anything else. In this respect, we in fact restore a kind of coherency to experience by noting that when things are illusions, different expectations are appropriate to them than are appropriate to their non-illusory counterparts: we can pick apples off trees but not off reflections of trees. But let us revert to our distinction. What of illusory experiences, where, unlike the examples just considered, I experience not illusions, but rather nothing at all: where it is only an *illusion that I experience*? This would be the case when I suffer hallucination, for example. Here I experience nothing, but I *seem to be* experiencing something, a dagger say. And surely the realist will not wish to say that there are hallucinatory daggers in the world. No. But he does wish to say that there are hallucinated individuals. Does this not really evade the issue, the question being how the hallucinated individual should know that he is so when he is so? In this crucial case— which is after all the lever by which representationalism was able to lift ideas off the surface of the world and open, thus, a distance between the world and them—there cannot be an instrinsic mark; if there were, I should be able to tell by it that I were hallucinated. Even if there were a mark, *it* might be hallucinatory, the problem being essentially how I should trust it. No intrinsic mark can hope to turn the trick. But neither will a mere criterion of coherency, since incoherency with a body of experience, while it is a criterion for non-genuine experiences, cannot serve to distinguish between experiences of illusions and illusory experiences. So something further than mere incoherency is wanted to distinguish the two cases. And a natural suggestion is this: the hallucinatory dagger, in contrast with an illusion, is not in the world at all. This is what the realist may say. He may say: the hallucination is "in the mind" in the sense that, though a hallucinated individual is in the world, the hallucinatory object is merely "in him." Here the realist is al- most committed by his theory to make a metaphysical distinction, albeit a metaphysical distinction we often make spontaneously, whereas the phenomenalist, with his penchant for neutrality, wishes to make *none*. For him, the "objects of experience" are all of a piece, there being nothing intrinsic to distinguish illusory from hallucina- tory experiences. *His* thesis is that the content of experience is neutral to any such distinction. Here, then, the issue spills beyond the limits of epistemology. The realist may say, if he wishes, that he may have some problem in determining which experiences are hallucinatory or delusive. But at least he recognizes a distinction which neither of his rivals can so much as *frame*. And if there is a distinction here, neutrality is metaphysically misleading. Obviously, if there is a distinction, more than mere coherency must be invoked. And if there are two sorts of incoherency required in order to achieve the distinction, it is not plain that the phenomenalist can succeed in his pure empiricist ambition without abandoning his metaphysical neutrality. The issues, then, take us outside of epistemology, but before crossing the boundary, we must examine another aspect of the issues that divide the various theories of experience which we have been surveying.

25. A somewhat related set of considerations, of particular moment to epistemologists, is this: on either the representationalist or the phenomenalist views, a curious degree of security is alleged to belong to whatever statements we make in purported descriptions of what we immediately experience. It is as though we cannot really ever be wrong. Thus, on the representationalist view what I directly experience is an idea, say of a chair. Whether or not this idea represents its cause, i.e., whether it accurately pictures a real chair, in case a real chair is its cause, is debatable. If I say it does, then very possibly I am wrong. But I expose myself to no similar or comparable error if I restrict myself to describing not what the idea represents, but just the representation itself. There is here no room, of the sort there allegedly is between ideas and their causes, for error possibly to enter. My experience, it must be recalled, could be just as it is whether there were something *there*, in the external world, or not. So while my idea may vary in semantical value with no internal indication that it has done so, nothing of this variation may arise when I merely report upon the idea, making no external claims and no semantical valuation. But not even this question of external correspondence arises for the phenomenalist, and so, whatever advantages the representationalist may claim for his ability to describe his experiences may be claimed by him, and, moreover, he is not even subject to the sort of error, of inferring from experience to the "external world," to which the representationalist is exposed. Neither, we must add, is the realist exposed to this latter error, since there is, on his view, no inference from experience to the external world, inasmuch as the external world is, according to him, exactly what we experience. But presumably he, unlike his rivals, is *not* immune to error of any sort in describing what he experiences. The question is, since none of these positions can suppose that what presents itself in experience is different, why the realist should be at an alleged disadvantage here?

One reason is this: it sometimes is argued that, though it may seem to me something is red, and I in fact so experience it as red, it may *not* really be red at all. To this, there is a ready reply: the object of experience just is what it seems to be; no distance can exist between what seems to be and what is when we are speaking of the objects of experience. And so since what seems to be *is*, I can make no mistake in describing what seems to be in experience, for so long as I say what seems to be there I will be right. I can lie to others but hardly to myself. Even if I should be using words in some idiosyncratic way, I am again incapable of error in saying how things seem according to my own eccentric usage. This latter claim is perhaps debatable. Philosophers have lately raised doubts as to whether the notion of a perfectly private language is even sensible. But still, questions of formulation aside, it is plainly an interesting strategy to protect oneself against a whole class of errors by saying that the objects of experience just are what they seem. But can the realist say as much for the objects of experience as he understands them? The representationalist has pried experienced objects off the world. The phenomenalist has eliminated the world, or reduced it to experiences: the world, consisting of experiences, is what it seems. But does the realist, or can the realist, take advantage of this sort of maneuver?

The answer seems plainly negative. Suppose, for example, that the realist sees a certain tree in a very blurred way: a blur is what he experiences. But surely the tree itself is perfectly clear at every point of itself. *It* is not a blur. In admitting this distinction, however, does not the realist have to abandon his view that we experience reality neat, and must he not accept some distinction between what he does directly experience—this blur of green—and the crisply articulated, foliated mass which is the tree in itself, everywhere perfectly definite? Just here the concept of *seeming* becomes crucial. For what status are we to assign to the seeming which we apparently experience, since, *whatever* we experience here, it *cannot* be the tree! This is undoubtedly an embarrassment to the realist, and it could be taken as finally destructive of his position, making it virtually one with representationalism. But he has one strategy available which is "realistic." Can he not say that the mistake which the representationalist makes is in supposing that the *seeming* is an idea, and hence somehow merely *in him*, when, it may well be, the seeming is in the world: the tree really is what it seems, in the sense that it is a fact about the tree that it seems a blur? If his rivals can say, of experiences, that they are what they seem, why cannot he say that things are what they seem? Why should a tree not really *be* a blur when seen in a certain light or from a certain distance or under certain conditions? Why should it not be part of what things *are* that they should appear just as they do appear, blurred or clear, depending upon the circumstances under which we see them? And this, he may continue, is the natural, common-sensical way to look at the entire matter. Why should we strip these appearances off the world, and make the object something absolutely distinct from the class of its appearances, which the representationalist has made into (mere) ideas? This makes things themselves virtually indescribable, at least by means of terms we do ordinarily use to describe what we experience. And it virtually guarantees that things will be discrepant with our ideas, so there is no veridical experience at all. So the representationalist's problem is solved, once and for all, by default. Things cannot be like our ideas. And what then is left of the external world but a blankly indescribable "thereness?"

We might appreciate this residual "thereness" as follows: consider the admittedly stilted sentence "There is something which is blue"; the predicate "is blue" cannot be attached seriously to whatever is designated by the "there is something"—if, as the representationalist apparently has committed himself to doing, we isolate the thing as it really is from the class of appearances. But is there here not, perhaps, a fundamental philosophical error? Have we perhaps not just taken the referring expression "There is something which . . ."—an expression logically distinct from the predicate "is blue"—and what it designates as a pure "thereness" which is metaphysically distinct from the blueness we have predicated of it? In other words, we may have taken the bare fact of indicating something and transformed this into something which is indicated, a bare *something*, bereft of any of the properties we would ascribe to it. The external world, distinct, supposedly, from all the appearances which the representationalist has mislocated as in us, has only been postulated as distinct in virtue of the fact that "there is something" enjoys a distinct grammatical function. The grammatical distinction between the subject of a sentence, which is used to refer, and the grammatical object, which says something about what has been referred to, has been taken with a primitive literalness as suggesting that there is a world of things which are merely therenesses, and a world of appearances which *cannot* belong to them—since they *are* mere therenesses. But to admit that any of them *do* belong to things is to admit that things are, in at least some cases, as they seem. And with this, the representationalist has been caught in the toils of a powerful argument. His position reduces to phenomenalism if he retracts the "thereness," and it reduces to realism if he allows what is there to appear. So what seemed fatal to the realist, if met in a certain way, is rendered fatal, instead, to one of his rivals.

This dialectical exchange, the sinuousities of which we have been following, draws attention once more to the notion of "thereness," a concept which, if any, is used to connect language with the world. It is not to be wondered at, in consequence of our characterization of philosophy, that the three positions which have divided the theory of perception, or of experience, between themselves, should, in the end, be theories of how the "thereness" is to be appreciated. The representationalist has in effect sundered the thereness from the sensible properties of things, has identified the latter as ideas, and has made it impossible, through this separation, that any of these ideas belong to the thing itself—which is now just the bare "thereness." The phenomenalist seeks, instead, to explain it away, either by regarding reference to something logically external to experience as meaningless, or by giving, as well as he can, an experiential interpretation of it, *not* as a further *item* of experience, but rather as the coherency of a class of such items—thus a coherence theory of existence. But this leaves the realist's position to be distinguished from the phenomenalist's, and it may be wondered whether there is room for distinction here at all. For in identifying the thing (a tree say) with the class of its appearances has he not, as it were, distributed the "thereness" as the mere unity of these appearances, as a kind of binding element which holds them together, as appearances of the same thing? So what then remains dividing the realist and the phenomenalist? Surely only the manner in which they are to characterize the appearances. And this is a *metaphysical* difference and one, moreover, which it is exceedingly difficult to suppose that experience could help us to adjudicate. For, as is typically the case in philosophical theories, they will not make any difference to experience: or rather, our experience will be just as it is, whichever of them should be right. Theories of experience are no exception: they unfortunately take us *outside* experience, and in asking and in pretending to answer external questions about experience, and taking experience as their data, it is not to be wondered at that experience as such must be irrelevant to deciding judiciously among them. But regarding this a few words further are in order.

26. When the Verifiability principle first was enunciated as a criterion of meaningfulness, it seemed overwhelmingly clear to its proponents that the meaningful portions of discourse were made up of words which, if they did not play merely a grammatical role, derived their meanings from experience: a term is meaningful to an individual only if he has learnt to use it through having experienced that to which it applies, or if he at least knows to what sorts of experience it would correctly apply. To be sure, there was a distinction framed between the so-called logical and non-logical portions of discourse, and the former would have been regarded as meaningful by some criterion other than this; but it is hard to specify in any hard and fast way the logical from the non-logical words and, for that matter, as the distinction between analytical and synthetic sentences becomes blurred, so does the distinction between these two parts of discourse. But at any rate the paradigmatically meaningful terms were thought to be those which either could be understood as applying to the world on the basis of some experience, or which could be exhaustively defined by means of such terms. And for perfectly analogous reasons, *sentences* were counted meaningful only in case they either could be verified directly by appeal to experience, or else could be logically

related in some close and tight fashion to some set of sentences which could be verified in that way. These latter, so-called *observational* sentences would be built up chiefly out of the *observational* vocabulary. Observational sentences were basic in a perfectly architectural sense of the term: the entirety of meaningful discourse was, according to the verificationists, literally founded upon these. It is via observational vocabulary that a system of sentences derives its meaning, and it is only if contact with experience can be made that such a system is meaningful. The ideal language, the language which would be wholly consonant with these criteria, would be one in which every sentence either were an observational sentence, or were replaceable, without loss of meaning, by a set consisting solely of observational sentences. Such a language would fit the surface of experience like a skin!

It is demonstrable that, for any system of sentences—any theory, say—which satisfies exceedingly weak and undemanding formal criteria, just this alleged desideratum can be achieved. We can, in such systems, replace whatever sentences are not observational with sentences which are observational, with no loss of power. This has been proved in a celebrated theorem due to William Craig. But when Craig's theorem was announced it did not bring quite the glad tidings one would have expected. For by that time even the more radical of empiricists had come to doubt the feasibility of a perfectly empiricist language. This disaffection came, as it happened, from some rather intensive research into the vocabulary of scientific language, which proved to be surprisingly recalcitrant to observationalistic treatment—or at least surprisingly so in view of the sanguine, but naïve, expectation that science was more or less the making of observations and that theories were just somehow shorthand summaries of experience. It was grudgingly conceded that if science, which had always been taken as *the* exemplar of responsibly meaningful discourse, exhibited irreducibly non-observational terms, observationalism could not *anywhere* be insisted upon as a necessary condition for meaningfulness: for to insist upon it would entail a repudiation of science and this, while it would be an admirably heroic course, would have to be regarded as mad. With this concession, the steady heat which the verifiability principle had been applying to the traditional topics and theories of philosophy had to abate: all the old metaphysical questions, bit by bit, reclaimed their former legitimacy; and in the following decades came more and more to occupy the center of philosophical attention, which is the case today. Nevertheless, a great deal of clarity emerged from the enterprise of attempting to force all of discourse into its observational portion. What emerged was a increasingly delicate appreciation of the variously interconnected strata which a logical cross section of scientific (or any) discourse reveals.

Consider, thus, what came to be known as *dispositional* terms. To say, for example, that a body *b* is magnetic is not to ascribe to *b* a property which a single or even any finite set of observational terms will *define*. A body is magnetic if it behaves in a certain way, e.g., attracts iron filings. But it is magnetic even if it is not behaving in any characteristically magnetic manner at a given time. A lump of sugar is soluble, even if it is in fact not in any state of dissolution. So we say: if the lump is put in water, then it dissolves if and only if it is soluble. Again, when iron filings are placed in proximity to a body *b*, *b* is magnetic if and only if it attracts these filings. These are not explicit definitions of solubility or of magnetism. Rather, they are specifications of how, in case an object is soluble or magnetic, it will behave under certain test conditions. And it is far from plain that any set of specifications of behavior under testing conditions will exhaust the meaning of dispositional predicates. What we have, then, is not so much a *definition* as a *reduction*: a reduction is only a *partial* specification of the meaning of these terms, but the important consideration here is that a great many scientific terms are dispositional, and, moreover, insofar as they are not observationally definable, they are not eliminable from scientific discourse. Obviously, of course, there is a connection between dispositions and observation. And there is always the possibility of achieving a complete reduction, which is to achieve perhaps a complete definition. Finally, it may be supposed that a dispositional term has no meaning outside the "reduction sentences," as they are called, by means of which they are introduced. So observationalism, while somewhat dented by this class of terms, is scarcely shattered.

A more crucial case is to be found with *theoretical* terms. These designate, if anything at all, something beyond the possibility of observation. Such terms as "electron" or "gene" or "psychological complex," will designate entities which are in fact, if not in principle, unobservable as such. Yet they play obviously central roles in theories which can claim a measure of scientific respect. It is such terms, or rather, the sentences which use them, which Craig's theorem enables us to replace by the observational sentences of the theory, and it is precisely in connection with these terms that Craig's theorem appeared not precisely helpful by philosophers of science. The reason was this: theoretical terms make reference to states of affairs which, though unobservable, apparently serve an explanatory role in making plain the reasons why the observable phenomena are as they are. We observe certain patterns in the world and wish to know why they hold. Often it is the triumphant achievement of science to offer theories in explanation of these, theories which make reference to often covert forces or entities or fields. To be sure, such theories are tested by deriving from them observable consequences, and seeing whether these in fact hold; and there is no doubt that a theory is in abeyance until it achieves a degree of confirmation which is based upon observing states of affairs whose description is deduced from the theory. Yet the terms are not eliminable in favor of observational terms, nor can the theory at once serve its explanatory role and at the same time sustain the total observational replacement made feasible by Craigian strategies.

The status of theoretical terms very naturally remains a central topic in the philosophy of science, and we have perhaps already ventured too far into its territory. The important matter only is that it is the intractability of theoretical terms, and hence of scientific theories taken as a whole, to assimilation to a merely observational idiom, which is the chief reason why observationalism and the radical empiricism which it presupposes are no longer held to offer touchstones of meaningfulness. A more modest proposal is that while translation into an observational idiom is *sufficient* for meaningfulness, it is not necessary. All of this, however, remains somewhat peripheral to the question I am mainly concerned to pose. For even were we to grant that everything could go through according to the original verificationist proposals—assuming that we could achieve all we wanted with a language which was purely observational in science, or, which comes almost to the same thing, the phenomenalist program of translation of all statements about things into statements about actual and possible experiences—there would still be some crucial philosophical concepts, having to do with things, with their "thingness" and their "thereness," which would require that we go outside experience. The language of philosophy remains radically distinct from the language of science.

27. How are we to analyze the concept of a *thing*? The phenomenalist, with the recourse to subjunctive idiom which is his wont, may speak of a thing as a disposition to appear under certain conditions. The reference to *dispositions* here is by way of anchoring these appearances *to* something: we want somehow to speak of a class of appearances as all "belonging to" the "same thing". And we might speak of an apple then as a disposition to appear round to the eye and smooth to the touch. The thing (the apple) is, to cite Mill, a *permanent possibility* of sensation. But *what* is it that *has* these dispositions? We ordinarily refer dispositions *to* things, e.g., solubility to sugar lumps; it is uncomfortably like catless smiles to have loose dispositions, unattached, as it were, to anything. So in what way can a thing just *be* a disposition, or a class of dispositions? Secondly, what of the *conditions* under which these dispositions to appear are actualized? Can we, as it were, build in the conditions under which certain experiences are had as further constituents of these experiences? And if we do, must we not then specify conditions under which the set of experiences, thus amplified, may be had, so that the conditions of experience are always, as it were, beyond the reach of phenomenalism to analyze and, insofar as they are, phenomenalism is ironically required to go outside itself in order to achieve its analyses? Such criticisms have often enough been made of phenomenalism; but it *is* interesting that realism appears unsusceptible to the same inconsistencies.

The realist does not require any *metaphysical* distinction between the conditions under which things are perceived and the fact that they appear as they do under those conditions. The conditions of appearances, and the manner of appearing under those conditions—these all are equally real. And so far as concerns the *first* difficulty, the realist makes no effort whatever to dissolve things to their appearances. He merely wishes to say that it is a fact that a given thing will appear thus and so under thus and such conditions and that this is an objective fact regarding the world. It is merely a further scientific fact that sugar will taste bitter to the dyspeptic, or that sticks look bent in water. So they may. But is he better able than the phenomenalist to say what the thing *is* (really) which appears variously under various conditions? Is the thing *distinct* from its ways of appearing? Or is it *just* the class of its appearances? And if it is the latter, in what respect has the realist given us a more satisfactory account than the phenomenalist, who speaks of an object as the class of its appearances? And if it is the former, well, what is the thing when we detach from "it" the class of its appearances? Granted, there is an advantage in that the realist is committed to nothing like the double standard which plagues the phenomenalist with the concept of "conditions." Still, regarding the analysis of *things*, can we differentiate the two positions other than with regard to the metaphysical differences which divide them over the status of appearances?

But once more, we must see, this is not a difference which shows up on the *surface* of experience. The realist may say that a thing is what it appears to be under conditions accepted as perceptually normal or optimal. The phenomenalist may say the thing is identified with a class of appearances taken as criterial. The realist may say that things appear other than they are under specifiable optical conditions. The phenomenalist may speak of certain appearances as "mere" appearances of the "thing." Both can in a way invoke all the same law-like connections. If this is so, what is left save a metaphysical difference?

28. It must now flatly be stated that the theories of experience will never be decided among on the basis of experience itself. None has and none can have access to any facts inaccessible to the others. Each is capable of giving an adequate account of the structure of experience, which will be the same invariantly as to

which theory of experience we may finally accept. So these theories are not at all like empirical or scientific theories. For, with regard to scientific theories, we do decide between these, ultimately and hopefully, on the basis of differential experimental outcomes. It is a banality of the subject that we test scientific theories by deducing observable consequences, and seeing if these consequences truly hold. And if they do not, we are committed to reject or to revise the theory. Experience is the final arbiter of what is true or false in science. We have no other basis, apart from internal inconsistency, for repudiating a theory—unless, as it happens, the theory has in principle no observable consequences. In that case it is untestable and inapplicable and, by empiricist criteria, meaningless. If we treated theories of experience as though they were scientific theories, there would be no way of deciding between them on ordinary grounds, since each is compatible with all the same facts regarding experience. Each theory gives a *total* account. So by the criteria of the verifiability principle, they are indifferently meaningless; and by pragmatist criteria they are equivalent, having all the same consequences for experience and making no essential difference in practice. Or, to invoke yet another criterion, espoused by Karl Popper, no *experience* can serve to falsify any of these theories, and if, as Popper believes, falsifiability is the criterion of scientific meaningfulness, our theories fall down badly here as well; or they do if we treat them as scientific theories. But if not scientific, what sort of theories are they? And why, if they make no difference, if they cast, as it were, no shadow upon the surface of our lives, should we feel constrained to accept or reject any of them? Why should we not hold them in aloof skeptical suspension? It is just such features of philosophical theories which the great iconoclastic and reductionistic theories of our century—pragmatism and positivism and Popper's falsificationism—found so frustrating and hopeless, and which they hoped, once and for all for the ultimate welfare of mankind, to have gotten rid of in such a way that the sort of controversies to which these theories give rise could never again come up.

29. Let me bring this out in a somewhat different way. It may be asked whether our experience need be the way it is at all. By this, I do not mean to ask whether the causal laws men have discovered in the painful course of millennia could be different, for they could easily be different. The world could show far different patterns than it now shows. Why should chickens not suckle their young? Why should humans not come forth from eggs, as did Helen of Troy? Why should not sugar, taken in oblong lumps, cure cancer? Why should men and women not procreate by shaking hands? Why should we not merely breathe in all the nourishment we require? Surely any of these things could happen, though of course much would have to have changed in order for them to do so. There is no reason why the world has always to be the way it is. But I do not refer to this in asking my question. I ask, rather, whether there have to be, for example, things at all? Suppose, thus, there are no things, no dense, integrated crass objects like tables and apples and stars and the remaining furniture of the universe. Suppose, for example, that the realist and the phenomenalist alike take their rise from a preconception regarding *things*: the realist being tempted to say that a thing is what, according to causal laws, appears to be thus and such under thus and such causal conditions, the phenomenalist saying that things are merely coherent classes of experiences; but *both* of them being driven to these theories, and perhaps even embarrassed by some supposed inadequacy in them, only because it is for each a foregone conclusion that some answer has to be given to the question of what a *thing* is. Do we actually *require* that there be things? Do we even require to think as though there *were* things, however these are to be analyzed?

Suppose there were possible a wholly different way of organizing our experience than the way in which we do organize it, viz., as clustering around certain fixed points, which we designate as things. I am asking a question which cuts rather more deeply than simply whether things could behave differently than they are observed to behave. I am asking do we need really the concept of *things* at all. Nietzsche, for example, proposed that it is purely *our* way of thinking about the world to think about it as made up of things which have properties and which stand in various relations to one another. For Nietzsche, things in this sense are fictions, impositions made by us upon the flow of experience, and which answer to no objective features of the world at all. Nietzsche contended that the notions of "thing" and "property" and "relation" belonged only to our perspective on the world, and that other, indefinitely many other, perspectives or conceptual schemes, are possible, and some amongst these might actually be preferable to our own. We articulate experience as we do, Nietzsche argues, in part because there is already a metaphysic implicit in the language we speak. We employ, thus, sentences typically of the subject-predicate form, and hence are spontaneously disposed to see the world as made up of subjects (things) and their properties. But with a different grammar, these categories might be replaced with others, and we should not even be able to entertain the *idea* of things or of properties. Our language, meanwhile, is what it is because we happen to have evolved in a certain way, and creatures differently evolved from us would perhaps have ordered the world in ways radically different from but unfortunately unintelligible to us. We would not know what they were talking about, or how they thought. And should someone within our own society happen to think along different conceptual lines, he would, through this failure of understanding, in all likelihood perish; so that language and social reinforcement hold us committed to the present scheme, to the categorial scheme of the herd. Still, Nietzsche proposed, it is in principle possible to break free, to achieve new perspectives, and in a way it may be said that his own philosophy was an attempt at this.

Nietzsche's views are rather perfervid echoes of the great teachings of Kant, who leaving it open whether other ways of articulating experience were possible, only ruled this option out for *us*. We could not, consonantly with the cast of our minds, intelligibly suppose that experience could be structured along radically different lines, for the lines along which we structure it specify the conditions of intelligibility for creatures such as us. Kant argues that these principles are not *derived* from experience and they logically could not be supposed as derived from experience. They could not be because nothing could be antecedently counted as experience which failed already to conform with these: these constitute, as it were, the logical shape of experience. One such principle, he claimed, is the principle of *causality*. Empiricists, and especially Hume, attempted to derive this concept from experience. But they were condemned to failure in this. For once again, it is not something we derive from, but rather something we bring to experience: *we* cannot conceive of something being experience which is not causally structured. It does not follow from this that the world has one rather than another causal structure: the world could, as we supposed, be radically different from the way we find it, with none of the so-called laws of nature holding good for it. But still and all, it would be a causally structured world. The raw data of experience, again, could be very different from what we find it to be. But it could not be different in the sense of being causally unstructured. No causal law is, as such, necessary, no sequence of experience could not have been otherwise. But the law of causality itself *is* necessary in the sense that it is a conceptual presupposition of experience as such. The content of experience may vary unpredictably within the confines imposed by the principles of ordering that experience in which our conceptual scheme consists.

It is perhaps ingredient in this scheme that we require the elements of unity and of togetherness which are demanded by the concept of things. But if this is so, it would, of course, follow that it is *not a defect* in the theories of experience we have been discussing that they cannot give an experiential analysis of what it is to be a thing.

30. It may then be that the concept of a thing is something we bring, as it were, to experience; something without which we cannot intelligibly suppose experience could be possible. We do not, as it were, build it up out of experience, but experience comes to us already in the form of things and their properties. And this would be so invariantly as to which theory of experience we might subscribe. But in this case, those theories must differ not in terms of the structure of experience, but rather in terms of the material upon which this structure is laid. We cannot, then, discriminate amongst them on structural grounds, nor, obviously, can we discriminate amongst them on the basis of any feature internal to experience as it is had by us. So the disagreement amongst these schools once more reaches an uncomfortable stasis, from which

there seems no logical exit. Indeed, the situation is almost exactly that of the representationalist, who could not peer behind the facade of his ideas to determine whether or not they were congruent with the objects he took them to represent. There is no way in which we can peer behind our experiences to see whether they are of "real" objects or whether they are "phenomena"—and it is far from plain even that we can attach any meaning to what it would be to peer in this way behind experience. Certainly we could not express in experiential terms what we might find. So it is not as though the standard criticism of representationalism is restricted only to it! It seems, indeed, to be the inevitable criticism of theories of experience generally: we cannot tell, in terms of experience, which of them is right. The question of which theory of experience is correct is an external question, which cannot be answered within experience. And in view of our notion of meaning, namely, that to know what a sentence means is to know what it would be for it to be true, it is a hasty, but not unattractive, view that these various positions border upon meaninglessness.

Let me attempt now to summarize what appears to be the dividing issue. Realism and phenomenalism are alike *direct* theories of experience, as we may term them, according to which, whatever may be the objects of experience, we have direct access to them. In this they contrast with representationalism, which is an *indirect* theory of experience, holding that the objects of experience are mediated by *ideas* and that such knowledge as we may have of the "external world" is oblique and inferential. The two *direct* theories differ in the characterization they give of the things directly experienced. At least I have tried to show that this is what the difference between them comes to. But the metaphysical differences run deeper perhaps than this, as may be seen by the solutions which each gives to such characteristic epistemological problems as those which arise in connection with hallucinations. These the realist may say are "in the mind." Phenomenalism requires no such explanatory presupposition as a distinction between what is within and without the "mind." But as we saw, it requires a very complicated criterion of incongruity in order to give its own account of hallucination. The *objects* of experience are on an equal footing, so far as phenomenalism is concerned, and curiously neutral with regard to any pretended distinction between what is mental and what is not. An hallucinatory object is one which merely is incongruous with received experience. But no *explanation* here is given of the incongruity, which, in contrast with realism, is perhaps a disadvantage. For realism can invoke all the apparatus of pharmacological science to explain why we have hallucinations. In compensation, the phenomenalist achieves a certain metaphysical economy. Instead of having to suppose two distinct *kinds* of objects of experience, some mental and some not, he can get by with just one kind, plus various modes of organizing these. And in view of this, he may argue, his theory is the one to be preferred. For, though both can give an explication of the concept of hallucination, his is the most economical and, at the same time, the one least committed to what he might regard as a dubious metaphysical distinction between mental contents and material objects. It then cannot be merely an arbitrary matter which theory we accept. We may invoke criteria of economy, as we do when we have rival theories in science. But still, economy would be a poor criterion if the theory it committed us to were false. And phenomenalism would be false if it were incompatible with realism, and realism were true, e.g., as it would be true if there were exactly the distinction it insists upon between mental and non-mental objects of experience. That, too, is a metaphysical question, and an issue to be settled there. Realism is a very natural theory. It is the theory we do rather spontaneously arrive at when we think about the problems of experience. But it seems to presuppose an immense metaphysical baggage. If there were no way of establishing its metaphysical presuppositions, then of course, we should have to question whether its naturalness should prevail against the economy of phenomenalism. And that would be a difficult issue to decide. But before concerning ourselves with it, we should say a few words upon what must impress the reader as a curious omission in what should be, after all, a discussion of the theory of knowledge: the problem, namely, of skepticism.

31. It must be stressed, in framing the skeptical question, that the content of experience would be the same however we should finally decide the question of which theory of experience were correct. It is this which tormented the representationalist: for his ideas should have every hue and texture they do have, and yet there be no world outside which they represent. The skeptic insidiously demands of him to show that there *is* a world, which is one with asking him to demonstrate that his theory of experience is correct—a thing he cannot do in terms of that theory, unless, as we saw, he resorts to the desperate, and in the end futile, expedient of ontological argumentation. So against the representationalist the skeptic has an easy victory. Indeed, skepticism here is almost nothing but a redescription of the representationalist's own position. For it must be noted that the skeptic cannot bring forward instances of illusions and challenge his opponent here to show that what he experiences is *not* illusory. For insofar as we are able to identify illusions at all, we obviously have criteria for doing so; any deficiency in these criteria exactly affects the skeptic's own use of illusions. The skeptic rather must be committed to the view that we have no way of telling whether our experience is or is not illusory—and this would be compatible with there being in fact *no* illusions *whatever*. He has to insist that even if there are in fact none *we* cannot tell that this is so. Skepticism, accordingly, is not an hypothesis which rests upon evidence, that is, evidence that men have been taken in by illusions in the past; for the position undercuts *entirely* all such evidence. Like a theory of experience, skepticism cannot be based in any evidential way upon experience; nor can experience furnish anything which will serve to refute or even marginally disconfirm the skeptical position.

We can bring this out in a somewhat different way. Perhaps the skeptic can at least draw from within experience illustrations for his purposes. He may take cases where, seeing a piece of mother of pearl, a man supposes himself to have seen a piece of silver. This gives him, as it were, a ratio: as the illusory experience of the silver is to the *veridical* experience of mother of pearl, our veridical experience is to . . . to what? Unfortunately, it will not help the skeptic to say to what our "veridical" experience may stand. For our veridical experience may be just that. We may experience things just as they are. Or we may not. Things may be radically different from what our experience would lead us to suppose. But then we cannot fill the blank in the ratio with terms which have application to experience. Since it is experience itself which he calls in question, and calls in question in an absolute and total way, the blank in the formula is a leap in the dark. We cannot say, in experiential terms, what it is the skeptic would be contrasting our veridical experience with. But he is not so much making a contrast as asking whether there is perhaps one to be made, whether we have in the end any basis for supposing that our experiences are truly indicative of how the world really is. But, as we saw, this is only another way of stating the position of representationalism. So the skeptic has in this respect not so much a victory over representationalism: he is a representationalist in disguise! Or he is so unless, instead of drawing an essential contrast between our experience and the world, he merely queries whether a contrast might not be drawn. For after all, it is a task of representationalism to show that there *is* after all a world external to our experience. To say that there *is* one, but that we cannot say how it is, is to raise seriously the question *how* we know that there is one; and should he say that in fact the world is distinct from and unlike our experiences, the skeptic must exceed his own strictures.

It was almost an express aim of Berkeley to dry up the swamps of skeptical doubt by collapsing the alleged distance between our ideas (our experience) and the world they were to represent. By collapsing this distance, no room would be left for the skeptic to occupy. The world just is our experience: to be *is* just to be perceived. How then can there be doubts? To speak of a world other than the world we experience verges on meaninglessness, given Berkeley's theory of meaning, and in this respect, the skeptic and the representationalist together perish into nonsense, each raising doubts which cannot coherently be expressed. Here matters would stand, perhaps, but for the possibility, which haunts us, of unexperienced things. While it may indeed be nonsense to suppose that there are ideas which are not *someone's* ideas, does not the fact still leave open the possibility that there are ideas had by no one known to us, no one except perhaps Berkeley's omniscient God;

and is this not the same as saying that there are things which none of us know about? So there is at least a world outside *our* experience? And if this is intelligible to Berkeley, what is it after all but an entry into the same set of difficulties he had hoped forever to remedy? For what basis in experience have we for knowing that, other than what we immediately experience, there is anything whatever? No *experience* can tell us this. And if we define, as the phenomenalist attempts to do, veracity of experience by means of a concept of coherency—our ideas are "veridical" if they cohere with others—we have then no basis for saying whether what we experience is veridical or not. We have not because we have no basis for saying whether there is anything for what we experience to be coherent with. The realist, who says in effect that we experience the *world*, that there are no ideas mediating *between* us and the world, can, perhaps, avoid these difficulties; except that *he* has exposed himself, through his solution of the problem of delusions, by holding that what we experience, when under delusion, is only "in the mind." For then the question is how we can tell, without going beyond immediate experience, whether we are experiencing the *world* or only something "in our mind?"

So each of the theories of experience opens up a possibility of skepticism. And it always does so at the same crucial points. Skepticism arises in connection with such words as "real" and "exists" and "true." And it is plain that what it asks for is that the suffering protagonists of the theories of experience attempt to define these terms in the language of experience itself: that there be some internal distinguishing feature of experience by means of which we shall be able finally to say that what we experience is the world. Not even phenomenalism can escape this difficulty and this task. It cannot by saying that what we experience *is* by definition the world. For there are the incoherencies which illusions introduce: and so the world is defined merely as the body of coherent experiences—the "wild" ones do not belong to the "world." But notice what has happened here. These theories of experience, one and all, attempt to rise to the skeptic's challenge by attempting to define in experiential terms what really does not belong to them; and in effect each is an attempt to carry out the same self-defeating exercise of the ontological argument. For what is it but to treat "exists" as a real predicate when one seeks to establish some criterion within experience which is the experience of existence? And what is any of this except attempts, of varying degrees of ingenuity, to treat expressions of semantical value—expressions like "exists" and "true" and "real" and the like—as though they were descriptive of traits of experience? And this is a logical error. It is a logical error, thus, to suppose that *truth*, for example, is a feature of the world, rather than the value which a meaning-vehicle bears when it stands in a proper relation with the world.

But when this is seen, then skepticism disappears entirely as a meaningful set of questions. It does so because it is a mistake to suppose words which depend upon satisfaction of a relationship between words and the world, should be taken as descriptive of the world, or as descriptive of words. To be sure, there are dreams and illusions. There are mistakes and wrong inferences. But none of these interestingly support skepticism if we know that they happen. For insofar as we know that, we know and can tell the difference between dreams and wakefulness, illusions and non-illusions, correct takings and the rest. Such doubts have no immediate interest for philosophy. But there are not any other sorts of doubts concerning *experience* which are of philosophical interest. Or there are none except the questions of the character of what we experience, whether it is material, or mental, or neutral, or complicated in one or another way. But these are *metaphysical* questions and, typically, not to be settled within experience if it is the character of the objects of experience which they mean to ask about. They are *external* questions and cannot be settled, as it were, by internal criteria. Let us then turn to some of the deep questions of metaphysics, which, after all, we have not exactly been able to neglect. It is a curiosity of the theories of experience that we have been discussing that they almost entail metaphysical theories precisely in conformity with the structure of the hopeful strategies they use to outmaneuver the skeptic.

IV ≪ THE WORLD

32. Let us revert to the criterion of theoretical economy which the phenomenalist invoked in claiming to have the philosophically preferable theory of experience. Here the issue may be put thus: if we have a group of competing theories, each of which accounts for all the same facts equally well, and where there is no obvious way to decide amongst these theories by pointing out some discrepancy between them and the facts, then other considerations become relevant, one of these being economy. It is not difficult to see why this should be a relevant criterion once we have distinguished what is really in issue here from matters of thrift and of aesthetic taste, which are sometimes supposed to motivate the drive for theoretical economy, such as when it is suggested that men might have preferred the Copernican, in contrast to the Ptolemaic, model of the solar system because the former was "simpler." If it were a mere matter of aesthetic preference, simplicity and economy would count decisively for very little; and since, in matters of taste, there is putatively no serious argument possible, rival theorists could invoke a more baroque taste in favor of the more complicated, involuted theory. But, as I say, there is something rather more profound here than this.

According to a tradition, it was the medieval thinker William of Ockham who first advanced the principle of parsimony according to which, if we may paraphrase him, the fewer irreducibly different sorts of concepts we are obliged to employ in our theories, the greater the explanatory power of these theories. Ockham in fact is supposed to have said that we ought not to multiply *entities* beyond need. But this comes to just about the same thing: it cautions us against introducing theoretical entities, in order to explain certain things which could be explained equally well with reference to entities already tolerated. Suppose, for example, one assumed that there were terrestrial forces used in explanation of earthly motions and celestial forces invoked in explanation of celestial motion, e.g., the rotations of stars and planets. Perhaps there *are* distinct terrestrial and celestial kinds of forces. But it would on the whole be preferable if we could suppose only one sort of force could be used in explanation of both sorts of motion. Or, which would come to the same thing, it would be preferable, on the whole, to suppose not that there were two sorts of motion whatever, but just one kind; or that the laws of motion would be invariant as to whether the body in motion were terrestrial or celestial. We then could cover all motion with one overreaching theory of motion. There are differences, perhaps, but it is not necessary to attach any theoretical importance to them. Relative to the theory, they are irrelevant. And this is not merely a matter of taste. It is a matter of intelligibility. For the more seemingly diverse orders of phenomena we are able to bring under a single, increasingly general explanatory theory, the better understanding we have of what are the important and what are the unimportant differences in the world. We see, thus, that what appears to be a heterogeneity within the world is not, after all, ultimate, and that beneath it all, there is a homogeneity we had not anticipated. The fewer ultimate differences there are, the better we understand the world and the deeper our understanding reaches. Ockham's principle—"Ockham's Razor" as it has been called—essentially, then, is this: do not multiply *ultimate* distinctions beyond need.

Against this background, it is not difficult to appreciate the efforts made by theoreticians of every sort, in science as in philosophy, to extend as far as they can whatever principles of explanation appear to have worked within a given domain. Hopefully, it can with slight modification, if any, cover another domain and perhaps another, until the boundaries between the domains in effect break down or dissolve. For when the same principle covers two heretofore distinct domains of phenomena, then it is as though there were only one real domain, the erstwhile boundary having stood only through the lack of an explanatory principle of adequate scope and power to obliterate it entirely away. But systematically executed, the hope is that all boundaries finally may yield in this way, until the entirety of existence may be taken as of one uniform piece, one seamless fabric however variegated and diversified and delightful its surface markings. But along with this goes the feeling that any boundaries we are obliged at a given time to countenance are only temporary, and a function of our relative ignorance. Of course, there may *be* ultimate distinctions and divisions within existence. But insofar as they are there, there is an ultimate surd at the heart of things. For we will be able only finally to understand what is the case *within* the domains thus divided, but never the connections *between* them. Indeed, it is not plain that there could *be* any connection, for to suppose one is in effect to suppose there is some principle which exhibits the connection, and which hence transcends the boundary. Insofar as there are ultimate divisions, the world is insofar unintelligible *as a whole*. Understood in these terms, it is not difficult to see why *ultimate* economy should be a desired trait for theories otherwise indiscernible.

33. In order to have a guiding structure for our discussions, let us think at this point of the sort of deductive system of propositions familiar to us all in the geometry we learn in grade school. There is, as we know, a basic division amongst the sentences, or propositions, which constitute such a system. These are axioms or theorems. Within the system, the theorems are *proven*, they *follow*, presumably by purely logical devices, from the axioms. The axioms, within that same system, are not proven. They express, we might say, the fundamental laws for whatever domain the system may be applied to, and they explain all the secondary laws of that (or those) domain(s), if we suppose the theorems to be these. Historically, the great deductive system of Euclid integrated into a single body many known laws of geometry, e.g., the theorem of Pythagoras, and when they were brought together in this way, a great many heretofore unknown secondary laws were discovered and deduced as simple consequences of the system. The principle of the deductive system is this: to generate all the propositions true of a given domain from the least number possible of assumptions or unproved propositions. The fewer the number of unproven propositions consonant with this general aim, the better. And it is not difficult to understand why the form of the deductive system should have been regarded as the preferred form for the exhibition of scientific theories generally, the hope always having been to explain as much as one could explain of the structure of a given domain with the fewest *un*explained notions one can get on with. So, though there are recognized limitations, and subtle controversies surrounding the matter, the axiomatization of scientific theories is on the whole regarded a desirable thing.

Somewhat parallelling the division of deductive systems into axioms and theorems, there is a division within the *vocabulary* of the system, that is, within the set of terms which are used by the propositions of the system. In a rigorous presentation of a deductive system, great care is exercised in the introduction of the terms to be used: one wishes to be sure that there are no notions of relevance to one's proofs which are not made explicit. For insofar as one is making unconscious appeal to background notions, it is not clear that the theorems follow by logical mechanisms alone from the chosen axioms. Now some terms are defined explicitly by means of others. Here definition corresponds roughly to logical deduction in the case of propositions. And just as not every proposition in a system can be proven, or deduced, so not every term can be defined. Some terms, accordingly, are undefined or *primitive*; and as the axioms express the fundamental laws, so to speak, for a given domain, so the primitive terms express the fundamental *concepts* for that domain. Since all the concepts pertinent to that domain must be expressed either by the primitive terms, or by other terms explicitly defined by means of these, it is again a desideratum that there be as few primitive or undefined (unexplained, as it were) concepts as is consonant with giving a total description of the domain being systematized.

One criterion of primitivity, either for propositions or for terms, is *independence* of the remaining propositions or terms of a system. The axioms of a system are independent in the respect that they cannot be deduced from one another. If a proposition is both required for structuring a domain, and is independent in this sense of the other propositions required, it follows that, without it, our understanding of that domain would be impoverished. But when a pair of propositions are independent, we must resign ourselves to the fact that they *cannot be explained* in terms of one another, and hence, the more independent propositions we require, the more we must admit to be unexplained in the domain. If *everything* were independent, *nothing* could be explained. And exactly comparable considerations bear upon the vocabulary; if all our concepts were primitive, no analytical understanding would be possible. So in as far as explanation and understanding are desiderata, there is a natural ambition to reduce to a minimum the number of independent propositions and terms (or laws and concepts) required for the structuring of a given domain. This leads, often, to the adoption of highly unintuitive axioms, or exceedingly unnatural-seeming concepts, which are justified if they manage to induce conceptual economy into a system. Euclid proposed that the axioms be "self-evident," that they would be assented to by any rational man, that one could not at once understand and deny them. It was for this reason that the independence of the celebrated Parallel postulate was doubted for so long a time—it seemed somehow insufficiently "self-evident"—and when it finally was shown to be independent, the requirement of "self-evidence" or "intuitiveness" was shattered as a by-product of the non-Euclidean geometries. For after all, these were demonstrably self-consistent but inconsistent with *one another*—and self-evidence is a shaky criterion if *each* of a set of mutually incompatible propositions is self-evident!

Philosophical systems have seldom been explicitly elaborated as deductive systems—the great work of Spinoza is a curious exception—but philosophers have been much, and justifiably, preoccupied with questions of *reduction*: with determining what is the least number of primitive concepts, and hence the least number of distinct and independent kinds of entities, we may suppose the universe to be made up of. As with epistemologists, for whom experience remains what it is, whatever theory of experience is adopted, so with metaphysicians, the surface of the universe remains just as it does, whichever *theory* of the universe we adopt. But still, within the universe, some things may be more fundamental than others, in the sense that *a* is more fundamental than *b* if *b* may be understood through *a* but not conversely. Obviously, *a* and *b* are equally fundamental if they are totally independent, i.e., if they cannot be understood through one another. And they are equally fundamental and *ultimate* if there is nothing through which either of them can be understood. If *a* and *b*, though independent of one another, can equally be understood through *c*, then *c* is more fundamental than either of them. Philosophers, then, are much concerned with finding the least number of ultimate and fundamental kinds of things required for the understanding of the universe *as a whole*, and accordingly, the sort of economy, which phenomenalism, for example, promises, is of a very natural interest to philosophers. Any proposed economy along these lines is a prima-facie reason for taking seriously the philosophy which proposes it. For if successful, it will reduce the number of *essentially* unexplainable, or essentially un-understood distinctions. It is hardly to be wondered at that philosophy should, almost at the beginning, have been characterized as a search for definitions. For when we have a *real* definition of the sort proposed by Socrates, we will have explained the nature of something in terms of something else, and hence have reduced the number of primitive concepts. Or again, insofar as one can prove, as Moore attempted to do with "good," that a given concept is *unanalyzable*, then, insofar as there are instances which exemplify that concept, we must resign ourselves to an irreducible, and hence a not further explainable, component in the final inventory of the world.

34. In the idiom of traditional philosophy, these questions would have been discussed in terms of *substances*; and issues of economy would have been appreciated as proposals to reduce the least number of independent substances we are constrained to suppose the universe contains. The concept of substance is a curious and technical one, and a few words must be said in hopeful clarification of it. It seems, undoubtedly, remote from contemporary concerns, but, admit it or not, the features conceptually associated with substances are at the root of so many of what are taken to be philosophical problems by our contemporaries that they almost comically exemplify the principle once stated by Santayana, that those who do not know the history of philosophy are condemned to repeat it. Only here, the repetition takes on an almost neurotic quality, as we shall see, for the repetition-compulsion of the neurotic consists in his perpetual and perhaps symbolic re-enactment of an episode he has long since displaced into his unconscious. So it is with this concept, as I shall show. This does not mean that the problems are not genuine so much as it does that they arise in part from our retaining something like the concept of substance in our general conceptual scheme. Whether it is eliminable from that is, of course, a separate question.

Substance, as a concept (or a conceptual requirement) served a good many purposes. To begin with, it was required not so much to explain changes as to render, in a way, the phenomenon of change intelligible. Consider, to use a celebrated example of Descartes, a block of beeswax which, redolent of the smell of honey, solid to the touch, sounding with that characteristic hollow noise when tapped, yellowish in color, has been left for a period by a fire. Here the block melts, changing as it were, into a puddle of waxiness, losing its former scents and colors and sounds and feels. There has been an exchange of one set of properties for another. Nevertheless, we do not suppose that one entity has been replaced with another entity, e.g., as if one were to remove a hat from a table and replace it with a bottle. Rather, there has been a change in *one and the same thing*. The sets of properties which have followed one another belong, after all, to the same thing, the change in which may be described by saying that it first had the one set of properties, and then the other. But then what is the *same thing* which we speak of as having changed? What is *the piece of wax* which has undergone this transformation? Obviously, we cannot identify it with either set of properties, for it is *the piece of wax* whether it has the properties, as at first, or lacks them, as at the last. So it appears to be distinct from the properties at either terminus of the change, and there is an overwhelming temptation to think of there being something, which *is* the piece of wax, which does *not* change. Briefly, if x is F at time t-1 and x is G at time t-2, and F and G are distinct and mutually exclusive properties, it seems natural to think of x as distinct from its properties and to think of x as just the same whether it has F or whether it lacks F and has G instead. So the concept of substance enters in virtue of an apparent necessity to refer changes to something (viz., *something* has to undergo the change) but, in order for the change to be referred to *it*, it itself must remain the same *through* the change which it undergoes; and it itself cannot change through this, for then it would not be the same (self-identical) thing which underwent the change. Literally, *sub*-stance *stands beneath*, remains constant under, the shifting properties which appear to belong to one process.

Whether, in this sense, there are substances, or whether, even if there are in fact none, we are required to think as though there *were* substances if we are to speak intelligibly of change—these are difficult, moot questions. Philosophers sometimes have spoken as though we are required to use a concept of substance, whether there are substances in the world or not, so that something like this concept is an inexpungeable element in our conceptual apparatus. It would at least have been this which Nietzsche was denying in his radical nihilistic proposal that there is no one conceptual scheme in terms of which we or anyone, are required to think; and that our apparent reliance on substantial notions is due, as much as anything, to the subject-predicate form of speech and the logical principle that contrary predicates can both be true of the *same* thing at different times. A different logic, or a different grammar, would perhaps enable us to dispense with the concept of substance altogether. Russell once pointed out that if we reflect on the matter we do not suppose when we say "It is snowing" that there *is* something which *is* snowing: it is quite enough to say that there is snowing going on, without our having to suppose that there is some thing which we must refer to as that which does the snowing. Could we not then, in the general case, instead of saying "x is F" make do with "F-ing takes place?" And, regarding change, it is true there would be some awkwardness, but still, we say "It is snowing" and "It is not snowing" at separated moments during the day, without supposing that there is something which underlies this change, snowing at one time and withholding snowing at another? As far as integrating this change, could we perhaps not simply talk of successive states of the same time and the same place? Obviously, there are various strategies here, but the important consideration is that there is a conceptual knot, strands of which are represented by the concepts of identity, of time, of change, of unity, of subject and property; and it is at least feasible that the entire notion of substance is due to a propensity to literalness, a propensity to project these conceptual strands out into the world, as it were, as its most essential furniture.

Descartes himself almost makes this point. He explicitly introduced the example of the wax block at a point in his discussion where he had just offered an extremely abstract characterization of his *self*. And he is afraid that readers will be put off by the abstractness of this. But Descartes says that in case they believe they really understand concrete things, let them but ponder the example of the melting wax. What in their sensory experience answers to this notion of sameness and of identity and the rest? Surely these are judgments which serve to integrate (here I am paraphrasing Descartes) our experience, without there being anything in experience which precisely answers to them. And indeed, we would be required to apply the same concepts whether we were deluded into believing that there were a piece of wax there or not. So the *concept* of the "same thing" is required, whether our experience is illusory (as he was then supposing it might be) or not. The more we think about the piece of wax the more we understand *ourselves*, for it is we who use such notions as sameness. However concrete the objects of experience, we cannot intelligibly think of them save through the employment of concepts hardly less abstract than the concept of one's self.

Philosophers of the relatively modern era, Berkeley and Hume, were anxious to dispense with the notion of substance: Berkeley rejected "material" subject on generally empiricist grounds; Hume, rather more resolutely empiricist, hoped to get done with the *mental* substance which Berkeley was reticent to jettison. Things might, as Berkeley proposed, be resolved into ideas, yet ideas do not float independently about the world; they have to be *someone's* ideas, and so there must be a mental, or spiritual substance in which these ideas reside—a conclusion Hume found gratuitous. By eliminating spiritual substance, he effected, he thought, a *deep* economy. Why not get on with just the ideas, or the things which, perhaps, consist of these ideas, and dispense with substances altogether? It is these destructive tactics, first Berkeley's and then Hume's, of which we find later versions in Nietzsche and in Russell. Here the question was whether the concept of substance is not expendable after all, and not demanded in the philosophical inventory. But quite apart from its alleged superfluousness, there are some profound internal problems with the notion which will return us to the main avenue of our discussion.

35. Substance itself, plainly, cannot change. It *underlies* change, and it is put there underneath the change to give some anchorage to change; so we cannot, consistent with this, tolerate the idea that substance may change. Imagine that substance *did* change! Then for exactly those reasons we were led to introduce something which underlay change, we would have to introduce something else here—or we had no need to introduce such a thing to begin with. Hence either substances are not required, or they have to be immutable. The *only* change logically permitted with these is not the sort of change exhibited in the continuous melting of wax, but the abrupt changes which consist in creation and annihilation. But furthermore, whatever properties characterize the substance must *always* characterize it: it cannot gain or lose these without being annihilated. It follows that those properties which substance can gain or lose without being a different substance than it is are not properties which really characterize it. In this respect the set of properties which the piece of wax has at the beginning, and the set which it has at the end of the change, do not really characterize the piece of wax as such: if they did so, the loss of the one set would be the annihilation of the substance; and the gain of the other would be the creation of something wholly new, and this would not be a change *in* the (same) piece of wax.

These bizarre consequences require comment, for it seems curious (at least) to introduce the notion of substance, in order to make change intelligible, and then to dissociate the change— i.e., the sequence of properties in which the change consists—

from the substance supposedly underlying them. But it was traditional to distinguish those properties held to be *essential* to a substance from those properties held to be inessential, or *accidental*. Accidental properties are those which a substance may lose or gain and yet remain the very same substance which it is. But essential properties are those which are the very nature of the substance. To lose these would be, in effect, to stop being; for the loss of an essential property is merely the annihilation of the substance whose nature is defined by the essential property. Here we make contact again with notions we have already touched upon: the essential properties are those we would have supposed required mention in a "real definition" of a given substance. For a real definition provides, ideally, an expression, which analyzes the expression to be defined, in such a way that it never is the case that one of these expressions should be true and the other false of the same thing. And of course it was only natural that the real definition could not mention accidental traits of something, since it *could* be false that a given accidental property belongs to something, and hence that the real definition would specify all and only the essential traits. In the pre-modern era, understanding was believed arrived at only when we had grasped the nature or essence of things, and hence understanding was a matter of getting a real definition. Once again, we cannot but feel that the distinction between essential and accidental traits, or properties, is a projection onto the world of distinctions which pertain to the nature of definitions—as though the world has to exhibit traits of a certain kind in order that definitions be possible or understanding be attained. Perhaps this is absurd. But until we bring into consciousness the various parts of this complicated theory it is very difficult to say that it is absurd, or to suggest an alternative view. In any event, we hardly can understand what goes on in a great deal of traditional philosophy without keeping in mind what would have been taken by writers as a natural and tight connection between definition, essential properties, and substances.

Let me illustrate this once more from Descartes. Descartes supposed, for the express purpose of attaining (if he could attain) the certitude he believed indispensable to science, that if a sentence *could* be *false*, then it *was* false: that if there were any ground for doubting it to be true, then one *might as well* regard it as false. So long as ground for doubt remained, how could we claim knowledge? Descartes held to an exactly analogous principle in his metaphysics, namely, that if a substance *s might not* have the property *F*, then it *is* not *F*. Thus the wax is yellow, but it might not have been, and still it would have been wax. So the yellowness is not really essential to the wax and, for strict purposes of understanding what the wax *really* is, the wax (really) is not yellow. This is then only an echo of the distinction between essence and accident. But Descartes makes an extremely clever use of it here, which we must mention. He first showed that it was possible to doubt that there is a world outside of his ideas. He could dream that there was a world, though there was not one. But so could he dream that he had a body, though, perhaps, he had none. But if it was logically possible he could dream, and yet not have a body, having a body was not essential to him! Was there anything he could not think of himself as not having? Well, he could not consistently think of himself as not *thinking*. He could not because the moment he tried, he *had* to be thinking. Hence, whenever he thought: I am not thinking; his very thinking of that thought entailed its falsehood. It follows (admittedly as a kind of joke), since it was impossible for him to think of himself as not thinking, that *thinking* was his essence or defining characteristic. He concluded that he was a *res cogitans*—or a thinking substance. Descartes here could almost be treated as making a joke at the expense of a philosophical tradition which had as part of its working apparatus the machinery of essence, substance, definition, and real natures. But there is little reason to suppose he was punning, or was not in earnest. After all, if one can think logically of thinking as essentially distinct from any bodily process, and can define the essential work of the soul as the activity of thought, then the survival by the soul of the death of the body is a logical possibility. This would have been an altogether comforting thought to someone concerned with survival.

36. We find an almost pure example of the essence-accident scheme in a distinction which scientists in the seventeenth century, as well as commentators upon the science they were framing, found it useful to make. They would not have characterized it as a useful distinction, of course, but rather as a true one. This is a distinction between *primary* and *secondary* qualities—a distinction we find in Galileo, Locke, Newton, and a host of lesser figures. Consider, for merely heuristic purposes, a crude version of the kinetic theory of heat. According to this, the changes in temperature of a gas will be due to changes in the velocities of the molecules which constitute the gas. As their mean kinetic energy increases, so does the temperature, and as it decreases, the temperature falls. This explains, presumably, how a body can be hot or cold, but insofar as it is a good explanation, it follows from it that the molecules cannot *themselves* be hot or cold. They cannot be if heat and cold are explained in terms of the aggregate behavior of molecules in random motion. Indeed, from this point of view, we cannot meaningfully ascribe *any* thermal properties to the molecules: they are a-thermal. Again, suppose we explain differences in color (as we do) in terms of different wave lengths. Then, if there are bodies smaller than the smallest of the wave lengths associated with colors, there is no way in which these bodies can be colored. They are, and have to be, achromatic. We find then, almost as a consequence of some widely confirmed theories in science, that certain properties, like color and heat, which we associate with the sensed surface of the world, cannot be properties of the incredibly small particles of which we suppose the whole of matter to be made up. In the seventeenth century, it was believed that the world was composed of very small particles, atoms, which had to be colorless, heatless, tasteless, and the like. It is not merely that we can succeed in thinking of them as being without color, for example, but that we cannot meaningfully think of them as *with* color and like properties. So it seems to follow that the property of being colored does not characterize the fundamental stuff of the universe.

Well, if we connect these conceptions with the traditional philosophical distinctions, it is only natural to conclude that colors are accidental traits of the universe—which 'is' just a sum of very small particles, no single one of which can be colored. By contrast, every fundamental particle has certain properties without which it could not be; it must have *some* diameter, *some* mass, *some* duration; and since we (allegedly) cannot think of bodies as lacking these, the latter are *primary* properties. It may be argued, thus, that though a body may be too small to be colored, it cannot be too small to have a diameter: for to have no diameter is not to be a body. Or, to have no duration is not to exist at all, since an *instant* is not a unit of time but a device for measuring the duration of units of time.

These properties then became the essential properties in the eyes of the early framers of mechanical theory; and it was a simple matter for them to sweep the sensed surface of the universe off the "real" universe, to assign it a secondary and essentially an irrelevant status. It very quickly followed, of course, that since secondary traits are those which only the senses disclose, the senses cannot disclose the real, primary structure of the universe's deep components. The senses, which have always in a way been distrusted by philosophers, were here, almost in consequence of science, felt to be pointless for understanding the real world. The sensory properties then were not "real." So the old philosophical distinctions merely take on a scientific disguise in the seventeenth century: beneath it is the notion of substance and accident all over again.

37. It is not as though the propensity to distinguish essential from accidental traits, and then to rule the latter out as perhaps unreal, or at least real in only some secondary and derivative sense, has been altogether outgrown. Much the same sort of distinction arises, and much the same attitude, when we have what appear to be conflicting descriptions of the (supposedly) same phenomena as given by science and by common sense respectively. The physicist Eddington thus once concluded that the table he leaned upon, despite his weight was not really solid to the touch because, according to science, it consisted chiefly of empty space: it was made up of incredibly small charges separated by distances vast in proportion to their diameters. How could something verifiably so riddled with emptiness really be solid? Eddington concluded

it could not, that common sense was wrong and common language false.

Eddington's conclusion is hardly atypical. After all, there has always been some sort of conflict between common sense and science, and philosophers have insisted that the world must be radically different from what it appears to be. Keats once drank a toast to the confusion of Isaac Newton for "having destroyed the rainbow." This was a poetic way of referring to the phenomenon of prismatic dissolution of the spectrum into white light, and concluding from this that only white light was real, colors merely staining the blank achromaticity of the universe. And poets, who have some stake in rainbows, in the lovely sensory surfaces of the world, felt themselves relegated to an inferior status as propounders of illusions about illusions. All charms, Keats wrote, fly at the mere touch of cold philosophy (= science.) But many of us quite naturally feel uneasy about the discrepancies between scientific descriptions (which after all enjoy a certain authority), and those we spontaneously would offer as the common view of the world.

In recent years it has become almost standard philosophical practice to point out against such theories as Eddington's that, since we learn to use the term "is solid" precisely in connection with such objects as tables, it is, perhaps, pointless to insist, but certainly incoherent to deny, that tables are solid. In its way, this form of argument—known as the Paradigm case argument—is reminiscent of the ontological argument. For as the latter insisted that, in the case of at least one idea, merely to understand it is to know it to be instantiated, so, with the former, there are certain terms which, since they must be taught in connection with certain objects, cannot be understood unless there are in fact things to which the terms apply. But while this may chasten, it need not ultimately defeat the scientist. For he may counter that the same considerations which led him to deny solidity to tables now leads him to deny descriptive authenticity to ordinary language: if it is ordinary language which requires that there be solid things, then ordinary language is just meaningless. The difficulty with this riposte, of course, is that it then is no longer clear that the scientist can meaningfully deny that tables are solid. For what does "table," much less "solid," any longer mean?

There is, however, a better objection. It is precisely that the kinetic theory of heat, for example, was to have *explained* the phenomenon of heat, just as the electronic theory of matter was meant to explain why crass objects, such as tables, are solid to the touch. Instead of seeing science as merely describing a world beyond the senses, which apparently was Eddington's vision, we might better appreciate it as explaining the world of the senses by reference to unobservable structures. There is a logical point to be made here as well. We wish to have explanations of the phenomena of solidity and of heat as such. Now we could explain why a stove is hot by saying that it has hot coals in it. We could explain that a room is cold because cold air is being pumped into it. But suppose someone asks why *anything* is hot or cold: we cannot explain *this* with reference to another cold or hot thing, for the question would be raised all over again. Thus, either heat cannot be explained, or else it must be explained with reference to phenomena which are athermal: to which the term "heat" simply does not apply. Solidity *cannot*, as a general phenomenon, be explained with reference to solidity. In view of these considerations, Eddington's ideas merely undermine the entire possibility of giving explanations; they stop the entire explanatory purposes of science. They render science, as an explanatory enterprise, either pointless or impossible.

It follows, from this general requirement upon explanation, that the world described by scientific theories *has* to be different from the world to be explained with reference to it. If they were the same, then there would have been no explanation. It hardly is to be wondered, then, that the structure of the world which science speaks of is radically unlike the world we live amongst with our senses. But it does not follow that there is an invidious distinction to be drawn in terms of appearance and reality. We are not justified in saying that, since we have succeeded in explaining heat, or solidity, that heat and solidity are not real. That is merely a prejudice, deeply entrenched, to be sure, and almost as ancient as philosophy itself, against the senses. We find this already, for example, in the great Eleatic teachings of Zeno, who *demonstrated*, through a brilliant set of paradoxes, that since motion is impossible, arrows cannot fly nor swift runners overtake slow ones; and since our senses appear to reveal flying arrows and the swift overtaking the slow, the senses must be illusory. To be sure, one could have concluded: so much the worse for Reason, which provokes such paradoxes; but once more, for considerations so sunk in the psychology of religious thought that we cannot as philosophers hope to disinter them, men have held the senses and the body in a curiously low esteem.

We find Zeno's destructive theory against motion enshrined in some famous teachings of Plato. Plato's criterion of reality, indeed, was immutability: nothing real could change. To speak of change is, after all, to speak, as in the case of our waxen block, of something x being F at one time, and being G at another, when F and G are distinct and mutually exclusive properties. But then x cannot really be F. For, to say that it really is F cannot be justified any more than saying that x is G. Plainly, x cannot be F and G—for F and G are contrary predicates: *nothing* can be F and G. Since x cannot be both, it must be neither, since it cannot be one without, as it were, equally being the other. Hence there is no property F which x can have—or which x can *be*—that x conceivably can lose. So x cannot change. Since, meanwhile, the real x is neither F nor is it G, F and G must be mere appearances, not real after all. Change, then, is illusion. Reality is not. So for Plato, knowledge, if possible, must be finally of what is real, and hence the objects of knowledge must be immutable. It is in the later tradition that the (true) objects of knowledge became identified as *substances*. It hardly is to be wondered that, as inheritors of so confused a tradition of prejudices, the scientist should have wished to read the appearances of things out of the universe, to stigmatize them as unreal, or unactual, or some such thing! But words like "real," unless they have the homely contrasts of ordinary speech, e.g., with "fraudulent" or "artificial," are merely honorific and bewitching.

There is one further point to be made before reverting to the convoluted topic of substances. Had Plato meant to *explain* change

102 · WHAT PHILOSOPHY IS

as a general phenomenon, it would follow from our characterization of explanation that he would have to do so with reference to
something unchanging. Plato, who felt that change was unreal, did
not, of course, feel required to offer explanations here: if there
(really) is no change, there hardly is call for us to explain change,
but only, rather, to explain why we believe there is such a thing.
We are not required to explain to the dipsomaniac why the pink
elephants move so fast, but why he thinks he sees pink elephants.
But once we resign ourselves to admitting change as real, we must
admit that we cannot explain it by reference to change! This, indeed, was recognized in the great scientific revolution of Galileo.
He abandoned the earlier attempts to explain motion. He merely
assumed that motion occurs, that bodies at motion or at rest will
remain so forever unless acted upon: his task then, and the task of
mechanics, was to explain *changes* in motion, not motion as such.

When we have a concept which we must invoke both with regard to phenomena to be explained and those which explain them,
that concept perhaps is a category. Things, for example, and
change, are notions we require at whatever level we are speaking,
or which we seem to require; and if this is so, these are (at least)
candidates for *categories* of thought, indispensable components of
our conceptual schemes.

38. If substances as such are immutable, as they by definition
must be, they cannot interact. For what form would such an interaction take? We speak of *a* and *b* as interacting, surely, only when
there is some modification either in *a* or in *b* which may be explained with reference to the other. But what is modification except
a change? And if substances cannot change, they cannot interact.
It follows, then, that substances must be causally independent of
one another in an absolute manner. So the ultimate furniture of
the universe must consist in the set of irreducibly distinct substances that there are. It is just here that we may appreciate the
motivation of philosophers to achieve as radical a reduction as
possible. For, in a manner which is exactly reflected in our earlier
discussion of primitive propositions and concepts, the number of
primitive substances we must countenance exactly defines the num-

ber of unexplained (and unexplainable) phenomena that there are. Parenthetically, this same consideration would be pertinent to the reduction of conceptual schemes: the degree to which we can reduce one concept to another is the degree to which we can reduce the ultimate unintelligibility of things. If everything is primitive, naturally it follows that nothing is really intelligible, each having to be understood through itself (whatever that may mean) or not at all. In general, it is plain that the ultimate ideal is obviously a reduction to *one* primitive, through which everything else may finally be understood.

The view that in the whole of reality there is but one substance, one primitive stuff, out of which everything is essentially composed and through which everything is finally to be understood, is termed *monism*. Monists, if successful, will have made the ultimate reduction in primitive apparatus and hence the maximal economy in philosophical terms; this is, perhaps, compensated for by the corresponding proportionate complexity in the apparatus which is required in order to exhibit the manifest differences amongst things that are not essential, since, apparent divergences notwithstanding, they all are of a piece. After all, the philosopher is as much concerned to explain (or explain away) differences which are not ultimate, as he is to identify samenesses which are.

Despite agreement that there is at most one fundamental kind of stuff throughout the whole of reality, monists tend to disagree regarding the fundamental character of this one stuff. There is, thus, the well-known view that it is *matter*: which is *materialism*. According to this view, the manifest differences which the universe displays must finally be analyzed in terms of differing organizations of what is at bottom the identical material. The traditionally opposite view to this is called idealism, according to which the universe as a whole is composed of just that which we take our ideas and images to be composed of, that is to say, something which is vaguely mental or spiritual. This is an exciting and unfamiliar view. Materialism explains differences in terms of organizations of matter, and often attempts to enlist science on its side since, according to its proponents, science somehow shows how matter is organized into increasingly complicated structures until, at the apex of these, we find entities of the sort which we ourselves exemplify. Idealism, by contrast, relies not so much on scientific theories as it does on theories of meaning—it argues, along lines roughly familiar from our discussions of Berkeley and phenomenalism, that a term *t*, which designates an entity *e*, must be analyzable without remainder, unless it is already of the required sort, into a set of terms each of which designates an experience. Holding that terms are meaningless save relative to experience, it is only necessary then to argue that experiences are had by essentially mental entities, viz., experiences are *in minds*. So, whatever there is, either is a mind or is to be appreciated as the content of some mind. Materialists, then, appear to rely upon causal reductions as idealists rely on reductions according to rules of meaning.

There is, finally, a third type of monism, known as neutral monism, and according to this, the ultimate single substance of the universe is neutral with regard to any alleged differences between mind and matter, the latter distinctions answering only to different organizations of the same (neutral) elements. This latter theory was advanced by William James, but its traditional exemplar is perhaps Spinoza. For according to Spinoza, mental and material —or, more appropriate to the seventeenth century idiom, thinking and extension—were but different *modes* of the same substance. They were, as it happened, the only two modes accessible to us, but it is consistently thinkable that the one single substance of the universe should have infinitely many modes inaccessible to us. There is a refreshing departure from parochialism in Spinoza. The more conspicuous modal differences between mental and material should, no doubt, be of immediate and absorbing interest to us: but that these should exhaust the modal possibilities of the universe impressed Spinoza as unduly narrow. That one single stuff, in which everything is and through which everything is to be conceived, or understood, Spinoza thought of as "God—or Nature." This disjunction has exercised a fascination for speculative minds: it suggests either that nature is divine, or that God is natural, either of which views (if they are not the same) rejecting the ordinary contrast which would have been standard between the world and God. Spinoza's ambitious neutralism was explicitly adopted by those American thinkers who called themselves naturalists, for whom minds were as "natural" as bodies without it following that minds were nothing *but* bodies or bodily states, as materialists are prone to insist, or that bodies are decomposable into ideas as idealists insist is alone the intelligible view.

39. Monism is counterposed to pluralism, a view according to which, whatever price we may be obliged to pay in ultimate intelligibility, and however prodigal we must resign ourselves to being with our primitive inventory, the monistic ambition is unrealizable because there are deep, radical discontinuities which cannot be bridged. The number of such gaps defines the specific quantitative extent of one's pluralism, but the historically most important pluralism has insisted upon *one* such gap, and hence upon two fundamental stuffs. This is dualism, and though dualism is called for wherever there is just one gap in the universal inventory, whatever may characterize the stuff on either side of it, the dualism most familiar draws the line just where neutralists attempt to erase one, namely, between the mental and the material. Other pluralisms are defensible. Descartes, traditionally a dualist, in fact drew, in addition to the customary distinction between minds and material objects, a distinction between finite and infinite substances (the infinite substance being God). In the Western tradition, this has perhaps been the numerical limit on interesting pluralisms—it is difficult to think that it could be philosophically interesting to defend a theory of sixteen gaps and seventeen ultimately irreducible substances—until we come to the extravagant and baroque theory of Leibniz, for whom there is an *infinitude* of independent substances (which he called monads). Monads, like substances generally, are incapable of interaction; and it requires an immense ingenuity to frame a plausible structure along the lines thought necessary by Leibniz.

How to adjudicate amongst pluralisms is not a question to be gone into here, since we are obliged to be synoptic. I should think the general philosophical attitude must be this, however. If there are any gaps at all, we have paid a price in intelligibility sufficiently high that, afterwards, it little matters how far we indulge ourselves in plurality. Perhaps there are two, or ten, or infinitely many ultimate elements in the world. Accordingly, monists have bent their major efforts at preventing the one seemingly obvious gap from remaining ultimately open, that one, namely, which ostensibly divides mental and material from one another. This gap, which is the most conspicuous one, has in consequence been the great no man's land of traditional philosophy; and this use of a term from trench warfare to characterize it is in no respect misleading. For what we find, as in trench warfare characteristically, is this: massive, indecisive, and intellectually costly forays and raids back and forth across an essentially stable front. This has been the history of the mind-body problem, to which I shall address myself now, a problem it might be well to think of as not easily expressed save with reference to the old substantialistic metaphysics.

40. Without some awareness of the logical features associated with the concept of substance, one can hardly appreciate, much less understand, the extraordinarily curious theories which have been put forward to account for the connection between bodily and mental states or events. These are sometimes held, for example, to constitute *parallel series* of events, a bodily event in the one series being correlated with some corresponding mental event in the other series. Why should anyone hold this view? Only because these are events in two distinct substances, and substances cannot interact, so there can be, as it were, no event common to two substances, and events in distinct substances are parallel perforce. But if we retract the feature of substances which logically prohibits interactions between substances, the entire *raison d'être* of this theory dissolves. Yet so long as there remains this radical discontinuity which must, consistent with the concept of substances, be required to exist between substances, it is something of a miracle that there should be any pairing off of events in one substance with events in another. Certainly, no appeal is possible to a causal connection where causal interaction is ruled out. In the seventeenth century, the apparent correspondence between bodily and mental events was taken as evidence for the existence of God! God somehow guaranteed that the series should be parallel. Indeed, it was by exactly such an appeal to the harmonizing influence of God that Leibniz proposed to explain the holding together of his universe of monads, which could not, since they were substances, interact, and so the whole sequence of congruent events, which each lives through in independence of one another, is the exhibition of a pre-established harmony and the proof of a daily miracle! How could one deny the existence of God under such a theory? But once again, as the conceptual grip in which the notion of substance holds us is relinquished, the need to invoke the miraculous mediative agency of God seems decreasingly urgent. But then, once we are liberated from the idiom of substantialistic philosophical thought, it is not precisely plain what the philosophical problem is any longer.

The facts, or some of them, are clear enough. We feel pain, for example, when our bodies, or certain parts of our bodies, are stimulated, or acted upon, in certain ways. We wish an apple which we see on the shelf, reach for it, and feel satisfaction biting into it. We certainly refer to bodily events here to explain certain mental events, and vice versa: when we feel fear, or sexual desire, there are obvious and undeniable physical symptoms. Now, given certain theories regarding minds and bodies, this reference may be difficult to justify. Suppose, for example, as Descartes did, that minds are (logically) unextended, i.e., non-spatial, and that bodies are (logically) extended, and spatial through their natures. In view of this, it must seem, interaction is impossible: the mind is too small a target to be touched, and too ethereal a weapon to be cast. How can something so light as *it* affect something so crass as flesh and bone? Here, of course, we are being dominated by imagery, but it must be remarked that Descartes felt the problem with sufficient acuteness to introduce a special class of entities— animal spirits—whose office was specifically to make this mysterious contact. Animals spirits were, so to speak, metaphysical cones, verging on nothingness at their apex, and spreading out to some surface at their base. This way they could touch spacelessness at one end and extendedness at the other. But this is a desperate expedient. If the same thing, viz., an animal spirit, could be fine enough at one end to be mental, and crass enough at the other to be material, plainly we have a single substance bearing both traits which had separately been used to characterize distinct substances. And if a single thing then can have both traits, we really *need* nothing to mediate. If, however, it does not have both traits, then there will be a gap at either end between it and what it is supposed to contact. And since no entity can fill this gap which will not suffer all the same problems as the animal spirits themselves, animals spirits are a hopeless expedient: we might as intelligibly appeal to pre-established harmony and the miraculous intervention of a beneficent deity. So long as these are events in distinct substances there can be no casual interaction possible. When, however, the causal prohibition is dropped, as it would be when the concept of substance is surrendered, the mind-body problem in its traditional conception disappears. *With* the doctrine of distinct substances, it is insoluble. If one modifies the notion of substance so as to permit interaction amongst substances, the question remains why one requires vestigial reference to substance, save as a general designation for stuff, any longer at all.

What I am endeavoring to say is this: the mind-body problem is not raised by any features of minds or of bodies, but rather by conceptual features associated with substances, and with the subsequent identification of minds and bodies as substances. It is not that minds are *unextended* but that they are *substances* that makes causal interaction between them and bodies so queerly inaccessible. But when we then turn our backs on the concept of substance, the old agonies of materialism and idealism cease having the metaphysical importance one would have thought they bore. How curious a fact it is that a single such concept can induce tensions of a sort which give form to a whole history of philosophy! All that now would remain to the problem is the purely scientific one of finding out what causal connections there are between bodily and mental events.

41. We must at this point glance at the concept of causality, which we have mentioned only in connection with the question of how the concept is acquired, if it is acquired. Here a few words might be spent upon its analysis. Far and away the most influential analysis is due to Hume. Hume proposed that we regard one event *a* as the cause of another event *b* only in case (1) *a* is temporally antecedent to *b*; (2) there is spatial contiguity between that in which *a* happens and that in which *b* happens; and (3) *a*-like events are constantly found conjoined with *b*-like events in our experience. Hume argued, with some force, that we simply do not know, save through experience, which events are related as cause and effect, and that, without experience, we could not tell, and certainly could not deduce from the fact that *a* happened, that *b* must happen. Since it is always a matter of experience which events are causally connected, there is no logical necessity in any ascription of a causal connection, and it is, accordingly, forever a logical possibility that the next occurence of *a* will be succeeded by some event other than *b*—or perhaps by no event at all. So it would follow from this that we have no antecedent certitude as to which are the causal laws descriptive of experience, and no internal guarantee that what are accepted as causal laws will forever be such, but we at least know that, whichever causal laws we do finally settle upon, the cause and the effect will have finally to satisfy the three conditions listed above. At least the *form* is invariant, even if the content is unpredictable.

Regarding *form*, however, Hume's analysis has been subject to criticism. Thus conditions (1) and (2) appear on their surface to be dispensable. In many cases, thus, cause and effect occur simultaneously. Hume had in mind the homely example of billiard balls knocking one another, and so naturally thought the first ball must move *before* the second one does. But water boils just *when* its temperature reaches 100° C; and though we tend to think that water must be heated continuously from its initial temperature to its boiling point, Hume has hardly the option of supposing it must do so: it could just boil when it is at that point, whether it reaches that point through a continuous increase in temperature or not. Philosophers, though they have raised the question, would probably concede that, within the present meaning of the terms, causes could not *succeed* their effects, so any temporal characterization which rules this out is probably compatible with our causal concept. The contiguity condition (2) is similarly moot. There is, thus, a celebrated physical law according to which a planet moves along its orbit in consequence of the gravitational force exerted upon it by the sun. This force varies inversely as the square of the distance between the two bodies, but there is no *spatial contiguity* between the bodies. This notion of "action at a distance" was particularly vexing to Newton, who felt he did not really know what gravity "was"; and theories rival to his, dominated by the contiguity requirement, supposed that there must be some dense material between bodies, and that gravitation is a continuous convulsion of this intervening matter. But there are other cases where it is at the least awkward to speak of spatial contiguity at all. Thus I may think of my wife when I think of a rose, and perhaps think of her because I think of a rose; and while this might not be the cause of the latter thought, the fact is there seems no prima-facie absurdity in my explaining a thought as happening because another thought did. So this leaves merely condition (3), namely, the condition of constant conjunction. And the question is whether this is actually enough?

We sometimes suppose that a given event would take place if another event did, that the latter would be the cause of the former, though neither event as such, nor any event sufficiently similar to either to make Hume's analysis feasible, has ever in our experience taken place. We believe that, in consequence of a very powerful nuclear explosion, the earth would be destroyed. Certainly, there is no constant conjunction of like event with like event here, and few are willing to trust to experiment to see whether anything like this would be so. Hence perhaps constant conjunction is not a necessary condition for a causal ascription. But even supposing this might be ironed out, the question would remain whether it was *more* than (just) a necessary condition. Thus certain events are constantly conjoined—the stock example is the alternation of day and night—and we do not regard these as cause and effect. It has been suggested that one reason for our hesitancy is that we require, before describing something as cause, that it *make happen* its effect. Day does not make happen the coming of night, any more (or any less) than night makes happen the ending of the day. The question posed by this, of course, is how we are to appreciate this further notion of "making something happen." Hume offered a psychological analysis. His view was that, as two events are experienced as constantly conjoined, a mental habit is built up. So, experiencing the first event on a new occasion, the mind, as it were, strains in anticipation of the second; and it is this mental straining which we then unwittingly transplant from our minds into the world, and read it thenceforward as that extra dynamic component of causation which the expression "making something happen" from now on is supposed to describe. But there is, Hume wished to say, nothing objectively experienced, apart from the constant conjunction, which objectively answers to this extra thrust we think is required in order for an event to be a cause.

Ingenious as Hume's theory regarding mental habit is, it must almost certainly be false. To begin with, it cannot be true that most of the causal information I have goes with a mental habit which I have built up through repeated exposure to ordered pairs of events. Moreover, when there is an exposure to repeated pairs of events, it is not likely I will count them as related as cause to effect. Thus I might hear for years a certain step on the walk, which I know is that of my wife, and then expect her appearance at the window: and while there is no doubt some connection, I should hesitate to say that the step which I hear caused her to be present at the window subsequently. Nevertheless, no generally accepted analysis of the missing dynamic factor has been forthcoming; and I think there is some prima-facie basis for supposing in the end that Hume's general view that cause and effect can be analyzed, so far as we can go in the matter, into constant conjunctions of like events, is very likely an ultimately correct theory. Hume, perhaps tongue-in-cheek—for he was, as Strawson has said, the ironist of modern philosophy—said that it is the best *we* can find, that the deep and hidden causes, the "secret springs," are forever inaccessible to *us*. But it is not plain that we can make much sense of this. True, we may find that what we took to be the causes of things are not, after all, their causes. Bit by bit, the devil theory of disease has given way to the germ theory, and comparable progress is always expected. It is, on the other hand, not clear that, however deeply we penetrate through the strata of more and more ultimate causes, that the *form* in which the causal relation is understood will be any different. Suppose, for example, that one says that turning the ignition causes the engine to start. There is a constant (enough) conjunction. But someone may plausibly argue that we do not yet have a causal account, for we do not see how the two events are connected; we only see them to be connected, without knowing how. Well, this is a request no doubt for an intervening series: the closing of a circuit, the production of a spark, the explosion of gasoline, the forcing up of pistons. But here, surely, each pair of events in the intermediating series is connected in a way hardly different from that in which the terminal events were. We cannot suppose that, between each adjacent pair, there is a further series, though of course, in any known given instance, there may be. But in the end, surely, we must arrive at ultimate causal episodes, paired events between which no intermediating event can be found. And to what can we appeal at such junctions except the bare fact that the two events are adjoined? Hume's theory, then, works best for the ultimate causal episodes, where nothing but constant conjunction appears capable of being appealed to. It may be, then, that this is as far as we can go with *our* form of appreciating the causal relation. But it is not obvious that there is any form other than this which would be intelligible to us, and, if this were so, then Kant's reconstitution of the concept of causality as a categorial component, brought to rather than derived from experience, would be vindicated. Hume would be right in saying that our causal laws derive from experience, and right in describing the form of the causal connection as it is understood by us, but wrong only in seeking to derive the *concept* of causality from experience.

42. Perhaps we can say more regarding the causal connection. We can say, for example, that, everything being equal, it would never be the case that *a* happen and *b* not happen if *a* and *b* are truly related causally. But this is saying little more than that they always are constantly conjoined. Our concern is not so much to pursue the refined questions which our discussion of causality may

have begged, but to point out that once one accepts that cause-and-effect is ultimately to be explicated as constant conjunctions of like events, nothing much remains of the mind-body problem save establishing what are the physical and the mental events which are constantly conjoined. This is by and large not a philosophical but rather a scientific task. What is important and exciting in Hume's theory of causality is the way in which it dissolves away the former a priori prohibitions against certain kinds of causal connection, e.g., between things of "different natures." Hume quite dispenses with this reference to natures, which is nothing save the echo of the substantialistic presupposition which creates the mind-body problem in its traditional form. Consider, in this regard, a curious theory according to which mental events are causally inert, that no causal connection may hold between mental events, but only between bodily events and mental events, so that, in order to explain the occurrence of a given mental event, recourse must be had to some bodily event. Schematically:

$$m1 \quad m2 \quad m3 \qquad \text{mental events}$$
$$\uparrow \quad\ \uparrow \quad\ \uparrow$$
$$\rightarrow b1 \rightarrow b2 \rightarrow b3 \rightarrow \qquad \text{bodily events}$$

Here the arrows indicate the direction of causality, and where it must be noted that no arrow carries us from mental event either to another mental event nor to any bodily event. This view is known as epiphenomenalism. It is a dualistic theory, in that it grants the existence of mental events, but it insists that these are causally impotent. It is difficult to see what except prejudice can precisely support epiphenomenalism. To begin with, it has no longer the sanction of substantialist theories, since it specifically allows interaction, albeit one-way interaction, between minds and bodies. But secondly, it is difficult to see how, if there should be constant conjunction between mental events, or between a mental event and a bodily one, we should say these were not causal connections. What would differentiate such a constant conjunction from a constant conjunction which *were* causal? Surely all that would differentiate it would be that here the mental event would be the alleged cause, and while it may be that it cannot be a cause, one has to do more than merely repeat the theory that it cannot be one in order to explain why it cannot be one. To be sure, it may in fact be the case that while we find constant conjunctions between bodily and mental events, we merely as a matter of fact never do find them between pairs of mental events. But this would be a scientific, not a philosophical discovery; and there is, at any rate, little evidence that it is true.

What does not remain altogether empirical is the question of whether there is an ultimate difference between mental and bodily (or physical) events, or between bodies and minds. That this is not empirical should pretty much follow from our long and inconclusive discussion of the competing theories of experience which, as we saw, had to appeal precisely to considerations regarding the sameness or difference of mental and physical events in order to account for the sorts of things we demand a theory of experience to explain. This being so, it is not an altogether empirical question, and perhaps it is not one at all, whether monism or one or another pluralism is true—however we are to consider these positions expressible once we have abandoned, in case we can abandon, the theories of substance which they presupposed. The best we can ask here is whether there really is an ultimate difference between bodily and mental events, whether mental events, for example, can be understood as just physical events of a certain sort. This very much depends, of course, upon what characterization we wish to give of mental—or, for that matter, of physical— events, and the degrees to which the question may be considered verbal must not be underemphasized. Nevertheless, in view of the central philosophical importance which the question appears to philosophers to have, we must say a few words concerning what is in issue.

43. Let us begin by considering what is surely the most economical of possible theories, namely, that mental events just *are* physical events. This is the identity theory, which in recent discussion has been defended and attacked with a certain understandable energy. Now the claim of identity theory must be considered rather carefully. Perhaps it might best be appreciated in terms of language, in the respect that it is consistent with it that our language for describing mental events should be very different, in as many ways save one as we feel it must be, from the language we use for describing physical events. This one respect is, at any rate, not a feature of language but rather a dimension of meaning. It would not follow, from the language being different, that we should be speaking of different things; but only that, in case we should be speaking about the *same* things, we should be speaking about them in different ways. Let us, in this regard, recall our discussions of meaning and reference, and think, just at this point, of a celebrated example of Gottlob Frege. The two expressions, "The Morning Star" and "The Evening Star" may hardly be said to have the same meaning, but they do refer to one and the same planet, namely Venus. To be sure, these expressions do not precisely belong to different languages, but they do say, or imply, quite different things regarding the one self-identical thing to which they indifferently refer. And it is this concept of reference which the identity theory appeals to. The expressions "mental event" and "physical event" may have quite different meanings without it following that they refer to different classes of events; and, if the identity theory is correct, they refer just to the one self-same set of events.

Questions of meaning here are very subtle and distracting, in that, if we do not quite carefully keep the lines clear between questions of meaning and of reference, we shall wander off the plane of discussion to which the identity theory is appropriate. Thus it is sometimes argued that it is implausible to suppose that when one of us speaks of a certain mental image, he should really be referring to some physical episode in the physiology of the brain, since we all know what images are but very few of us know the first thing regarding states of the brain. But this is a very poor argument. The ancients, in speaking of the moon, were in fact referring to the unique satellite of the Earth; but they would hardly have known that this is what they were referring to, since they did not know the object under this description. Here the argument will have confused meaning with reference. Again, it might be linguistically inappropriate to say something like "I am feeling a certain brain state" when the fact is that one is feeling a certain emotion—without it again following that the emotion in question is not a brain-state. It is only that two co-referential expressions might have different grammars, as it were, and fit differently into different syntactical contexts. The question then is whether we have good reason, granting that physical and mentalistic predicates are never synonymous, for supposing that they could not be co-referential.

44. In one respect, of course, we can answer the question easily. Thus we predicate "has an image" and "is in a certain brain state" of one and the same *person*. It may very well be then that persons are metaphysically susceptible of sustaining correct descriptions with physical and mental predicates alike; and there may even be some law-like connection to the effect that whenever a certain mental predicate should be true of a person, then and then only is a certain physical predicate true of him as well. Descartes supposed that persons consisted of a *res cogitans* mysteriously united to a *res extensas*—that we are a thinking thing darkly tethered to an extended thing—and thus may be thought to have held that mental predicates are true of one part of us, and physical predicates true of the other part. Yet we might say that there is no reason to suppose these predicates should be true of distinct things, loosely connected to one another, but rather, they might indifferently be true of one self-identical, metaphysically interesting sort of entity—a person—where persons are defined virtually as entities of whom these two sorts of predicates can be simultaneously true. Such a thesis has been advanced in the last few years by the British philosopher, P. F. Strawson. It is in general a theory somewhat congenial to the modern philosophical temper. A comparable theory was advanced somewhat earlier by Gilbert Ryle, in a singularly influential work, the *Concept of Mind*. For Ryle, mental predicates were analyzed not as ascribing to an individual a certain mental event, but rather as ascribing to him a disposition to behave in certain characteristic fashions. To say that he is jealous, thus, is in effect to say what in general he may be expected to do under various specifiable conditions. It is consonant with Ryle's analysis that such dispositions should be exhibited only by those individuals whom Strawson would recognize as persons. Ryle's analysis, however, leaves unresolved the criterion for distinguishing mental dispositions from other sorts, and though he might say that it does not deeply matter, from his position, that there should be any difference, the fact remains that many philosophers balk at the suggestion that mental predicates *never* ascribe mental episodes. It seems plain, for example, that we do have images, or that some of us do. If this is a fact, it is a fact, and it is never to a philosopher's interest to deny facts. Any solution to a problem has to accept the facts which constitute the problem, and while it may well be true that a great many so-called mental predicates are analyzable as ascriptions of dispositions to behave, if they all cannot be so analyzed, the problem is with us. Moreover, while it may be true that it is persons who *have* images, and though it may be generally the case that there are no images which exist on their own, it is still not true that in referring to images we are referring to persons. Rather, that a person is involved when there is an image may be a presupposition of any discussion of images, without it following that, in referring to images, we are referring to a person. And the question remains whether, in referring to an image, we are referring to a brain-state of the very same person presupposed as having the image in the first place. So, metaphysically instructive as the theory of persons is, it leaves untouched the deep questions raised by the identity theory. Or, perhaps, it only diverts our attention from these deep questions.

Let us suppose the identity theory were correct, and that mental and physical predicates, though non-synonymous, are co-referential. It is certainly possible that we should, as we saw, experience an object under one description and yet not know to be true of it another description, though the latter *be* true of it. The predicates "looks round" and "looks elliptical" thus may be true of the same identical penny. We may experience the penny in such a way as to know it to look round and yet not know it to look elliptical as well. So is it not feasible, at least, that I might experience the same "thing" as an image and yet not know that it is a brain-state as well?

To be sure, being an image is no more the same as being a brain state, than looking elliptical is the same as looking round. Yet if the same thing may, from different viewpoints, look round *and* elliptical, perhaps the same thing may similarly be an image and a brain-state at once. And this is all the identity theory can insist upon. Since, again as seems feasible, two distinct properties can belong to the same thing, one might know that one holds without knowing that the other holds; and, unless the identity theory wants to say that the two *properties* are the same, one can distinguish these properties while supposing them to be properties of the same thing. To be sure, this leaves a question of what ultimate characterization we should give of this "thing." We should have to answer "neither" or "both" to the question "Is the same thing physical or mental?" But this is a general problem of how *things* are to be understood, and much the same hesitant answer would have to be given to the question "Is the penny round or elliptical?" And here, I should think, matters would have to rest, requiring more a decision than a solution, were it not for the remaining question of the differences there may be between the pair "mental" and "physical" in contrast with the pair "round" and "elliptical." The issue is whether, however we construe "thing," the same thing *can* be supposed at once mental and physical, whether, in the way in which a penny can appear to be round or elliptical, something can appear to be an image or a brain-state. Is there any good reason for supposing that these traits cannot co-inhere in one and the same entity?

45. Mental properties or traits appear, for one thing, to be private whereas physical traits do not. In this respect there appears to be a difference between the mental and the physical traits which does not differentiate roundness from ellipticity; the traits which a penny has of being round and elliptical, or the traits which Venus has of appearing as a star in the morning and a star in the evening, are of a piece in this regard. How crucial a difference is this? I and I alone have access to my own mental images. Nobody could have my images, though others doubtless have images rather like mine, and, for all any of us can tell, some of their images differ from mine *solo numero*. Nevertheless, the image I now have

is experienced by at most (and of course by at least) one person (me). By contrast, brain-states, so far as we can speak of them as in the physical world and experienceable, are in principle capable of being experienced by a plurality of individuals. The question then is how images could be brain states if, in fact, it follows that the self-identical thing could at once be experienced by at most one person and can be experienced by several people at once? Or again, it makes sense, one would think, to say that there are brain-states which nobody experiences, but not that there are images which nobody experiences. This may be a good argument for demonstrating that images cannot be brain-states. But the question is whether "can be experienced by at most one person" and "can be experienced by more than one person"—which are admittedly incompatible—any more are incapable of characterizing one and the same thing than are "is round" and "is elliptical"—which are, after all, hardly less incompatible. The difficulty with meeting the argument in this way, however, is that it provides us with a formula for answering all arguments of the sort which attempts to prove that something cannot be identical with something else because, if it were, it would have to require ascription of incompatible predicates. This, perhaps, means that there is no way of refuting the identity theory, except by suggesting that insofar as it is irrefutable, it is not conceivably an empirical theory. But this need not faze the identity theorist in the least.

The concept of privacy, however, merits a brief discussion. If my immediate mental states are uniquely accessible to me, and if this is generally the case with each of us, a large class of epistemological problems is generated. There is, to begin with, the question of how we ever should be able to make the sorts of intersubjective comparisons which would enable us to know whether our experiences were different or alike or, for that matter, to find out whether others even have experiences. This is, roughly, the problem of other minds, as it is called. It is a particularly vexing problem when taken in conjunction with a theory of meaning we are familiar with by now. If I and I alone can experience my own mental states, I and I alone can verify sentences reporting on my own mental states. Since no other person can in principle verify these sentences they must, by the theory equating the meaning of a sentence with its mode of verification, be meaningless to everyone except myself; and, insofar as uniquely meaningful to *me*, the sentences which report my mental state must be, as it were, in a language comprehensible to at most one person, a language, in brief, which is logically private to him. So far as it should be the case that we do have mental states, none of us should be able to understand what any of us would be saying, and each would speak in a private tongue. It may be pointed out that in case we do understand one another, either mental states are not private (which seems wrong) or the verificationist theory of meaning cannot be right (which seems true). And as the verificationist principle is relinquished, the other minds problem changes its character. Nevertheless, it is instructive to observe how philosophers responded to the tensions to which it gave rise.

There is, to begin with, the physicalist approach, which is the suggestion that mental terms be tied to physical or behavioral criteria in such a manner that ascription of mental predicates is automatic upon correct ascription of physical ones. It is in this spirit that we must appreciate the radical behaviorism of Watson, where mental states just were stretches of behavior (thinking just was tiny laryngial spasms) or, more subtly, the later linguistic behaviorism of Ryle. In the latter reconstruction, terms which putatively refer to inner mental states or episodes must be replaced by, or, if not replaced by, then understood as though they were, terms which referred to actual and possible passages of behavior. Ryle made the patently plausible observation that we have little difficulty, and certainly no difficulty which is of philosophical moment, in ascribing mental predicates to individuals. There *cannot* be, in consequence of this obvious ease of description, anything which is essentially occult or utterly interior here; for in that case what we do with such ease would not be difficult but impossible. Moreover, if such terms as "angry," "imaginative," "jealous," "happy," are of this sort, then a man who denies that it is impossible to tell whether someone is angry must *mean* by "is angry" something quite different from what it means in our language. And in this case it is not at all clear that we can tell *what* he means. But at the least he cannot be meaning that we cannot tell whether or not people are angry in *our* sense of the word. And what other sense, really, can matter?

The main arguments against the possibility of a private language derive from Wittgenstein, whose point appears to have been (and what Wittgenstein exactly meant is a matter of continuing controversy) that anything recognizably a language requires that there be rules, and nothing can be seriously regarded as a rule unless there are ways of determining infractions of it. But what, after all, is to be counted an infraction or, for the matter, an adherence to a rule when the entire thing is up to me, as it were, as it would have to be if my language were private? It is not plain, I should think, that merely because a language were private, it would or need be arbitrary, as this criticism implies. But Wittgenstein's suggestion is that it perhaps could not be other than arbitrary if there were no public mode of checking up on the part of more than one person. Wittgenstein must not be taken as having said that mental states are not private, only that the language we use to report them (though he was uneasy about the notion of reporting) could be private. Ryle went to a rather more radical position in denying, or in reaching the verge of denying the occurrence of essential private episodes. Both of their positions, along with the rather vast commentary their rich investigations have elicited, are concerned, nevertheless, with questions of meaning, and if they are right, in the end, this entails at best a repudiation of the theory of meaning which makes mental predicates private, and leaves unaffected the sense that we and we alone are privy to our own mental states, and enjoy, in regard to them, a certain ultimate authority.

That we have this authority means that we are able to verify (insofar as we have need of verifying) ascriptions of mental predicates to us in a way different from, and possibly more certain than, the way in which others can verify these ascriptions when they are made of us. In many cases—and Ryle derives a measure of strength from these—this is not so. I am perhaps the last person in the world to know how vain I am, or even if I am vain. None of us is in as good a position as another is to determine whether or not we are intelligent, or at least in no *better* a position. But vanity and intelligence are uncontroversially mental predicates. Having allowed this, however, the fact is that we learn (though Ryle might point out that we *do* have to *learn*) to dissimulate our feelings, to suppress at least the outward show of our emotions, to keep our thoughts to ourselves, and to suffer in isolation our own inner agonies. We do this, but we need not; and the degree in which we do so is a matter of social convention as much as of anything. But more important, for present purposes, is this: others may have a different way of verifying the sentence "*m* is angry" than *m* does. They verify it by noting that *m* displays the manifest show of the angry man; *m* verifies it by knowing how he feels. But it is, after all, one and the same thing which the others can tell about and which *m* feels, namely, *m*'s wrath. And if this case holds in a general way, we might conclude that there *is* no difficulty in a feeling, which is private, and a bit of behavior, which is not, characterizing one and the same thing, namely, the wrath of *m*. And if this is so, there seems to be reason for regarding the argument based upon privacy as conclusive against the identity theory. We need not, in the interests of meaningfulness, deny privacy. Privacy has only to do with a mode of access to the same thing to which others have a different mode of access. The same thing may be gotten at differently without being a different *thing*.

46. When one speaks of an "external manifestation" of interior, or "mental" episodes, or when one speaks of there being behavioral criteria for the ascription of mental predicates, or when one proposes any variant of the physicalist program requiring all psychological predicates to be tied logically to physical ones, one has not, perhaps, as thoroughly canvassed as one should what is conceptually involved in the notion of "external behavior," as such. Philosophers have in quite recent times felt a distinction imperative between bodily movements, on the one hand, and what they speak of, on the other, as "actions." The question here is how we are to effect a distinction between a man's arm going up and that man (or any man) actually *raising* his arm. Obviously, nothing external will mark the difference if we believe, which seems justified, that the upward motion of the arm is invariant to the two cases. But it is not plain what interior event, if any, we would be referring to when we make the distinction we all recognize as a common one. Wittgenstein once proposed the problem thus: subtract from the fact that a man raises his arm, the fact that his arm goes up. What remains?

A traditional answer is that, when the movement of the arm is due to an act of will, or a volition, the arm movement is an action, so what would be left over, by executing the Wittgensteinian subtraction, is a volition. This view is not widely favored in contemporary philosophy. One reason for the disrepute of the theory is that, in view of the supposed frequency with which we perform actions, volitions should be amongst the most familiar episodes of mental life. But the fact is that if we reflect upon the matter in a candid way, we will find that we very seldom can detect a volition in any explicit way. I can, for instance, do some such thing as say to myself "I will make an effort to raise my arm"—a statement which will perhaps be appropriate when there are circumstances real or imagined which would be taken as causing some difficulty in raising that arm. But in general I do not make these interior statements when I perform the actions I presumably perform and, more telling, the making of a statement is itself an action. For we might want to distinguish, after all, between making a statement and merely having the words come out of one's mouth. And sofar then as making a statement is concerned, if *it* is an action, then, on the theory that all actions require a volition, it must be distinguished from its volition, and it appears to follow that *it* is not a volition. In view, then, of the curious unavailability of volitions, and of the logical inappropriateness of those episodes we are prone to take for volitions, the theory seems untenable. We *know*, after all, that not all volitions can be actions if every action requires a volition; for then we should have an infinite regression which would rule out the possibility of actions at all.

Certainly, even on the most charitable of interpretations, there cannot ordinarily be supposed a causal relation between volitions and bodily movements. For as a general rule, with many of the things we do, we simply do them, as it were, without doing something else—executing a volition or anything else—which causes them to happen. When I raise my arm, for example, I simply raise it: I do nothing which then causes my arm to rise. We all must recognize a difference between the way in which we typically move our arms and the way in which we typically move matchboxes. With matchboxes we must do something—pushing, say—which causes them to move. But I commonly do nothing which, in the same regard, causes my arm to move: I *just* move it. And it must be recognized that this distinction cuts across the ordinary distinction, however it is to be framed, between mental and physical, or bodily, occurrences. I can cause certain mental events to happen, for instance, by doing something else first: I take a drug in order to get an image. But then I also can *simply* have an image, e.g., if someone asks me to frame the mental image of a triangle, I can easily comply with this. Now on the theory of volitions, all actions, whether mental or bodily, would be examples of "causing something to happen." But then we could not cause volitions to happen, for we would then have an infinite regression. If, however, volitions were not actions in their own right, and if they were not held to stand in the relation of cause-to-effect to bodily motions, then we might find some different role for volitions to play; and the theory of volitions would then be subject only to the criticism that we do not seem to be able to say what volitions are, or how we should individuate them. And after all, what really is then left of the theory of volitions except this: they are that factor, whatever it is, which we feel must be left over when we subtract "*m*'s arm goes up" from the fact that "*m* raises his arm"?

Let us consider some other cases in which analogous problems arise. Indeed, we have already an example of one in the case of making a statement, and in having a string of words issue forth from one's mouth. Consider any sentence *s*. Imagine that a machine writes *s* on a moving tape, or that *s* comes out of the loudspeaker of a machine. We are prepared to say that the machine writes or that it has a sentential output, but we are not prepared to say that the machine *asserts* the sentence. Now this is something like the difference between a machine moving a certain piece, a rod, say, which machines can do, and a machine performing an action of moving a rod, which we are perhaps disinclined to say that a machine can do. But the difference between merely voicing a sentence and asserting a sentence can surely be analogous to *our* arm merely moving, and our actually moving our arm as an action. Suppose we somewhat extended this notion of *asserting* so that, one might say, a bodily movement, when "asserted" by him whose bodily movement it is, is an action. Now just as a sentence is invariant in meaning whether it is asserted or not, the assertion making no *internal* change in a sentence; so an arm movement is invariant as to whether it is "asserted" or not: the *doing* of an arm movement makes no *internal* change in the movement of the arm.

This analogy can be protracted. Thus it might be argued that, just as such, sentences neither are true nor false. They merely are certain physical objects: ink marks or sound waves. The very same sentential object becomes true or false only when asserted, and then it will be true or false depending upon who asserts it and under what conditions it is asserted. In a similar way bodily movements are not successes or failures, just as such. They will be physical events, having what consequences they have in a physical series of events, whether they are *done* or are not. Consider an arm movement of the sort one might use to attract attention. An arm movement could be of this sort without being described correctly as an attempt to attract attention. For the arm merely moved that way without anyone moving it. The same movement could have been done idly, without he who did it "meaning" anything by it. Or he may in effect do it meaning that it should succeed in attracting attention. In that case it is a success or failure, depending upon whether attention is attracted or is not. So the words "It is raining" may come out of a mouth. Or a man may pronounce them idly. Or he may *say* them, meaning to say something true. Then they are true or false depending upon whether it is raining when and where he says them or not. Success and failure are externally conferred upon action, as truth and falsity are externally conferred upon assertions.

Now it is plain that the assertion of a sentence is not *part* of the sentence. The logician Frege introduced a special sign, ⊢ , which was to mark the fact that whatever followed it was being asserted.

But the sentence *s* retains its meaning whether it is asserted or not, so that ⊢*s* has the same meaning as *s* itself has, only in the former case *s* is asserted. Nothing internal to the sentence tells you that it is asserted. If you see a sentence written down, you will not know whether the man who wrote it was practicing his hand-writing or leaving a message. Just as an asserted sentence is not a special sort of sentence, but, rather, a special operation with any sort of sentence, so an action is not just a special sort of bodily movement, but a certain sort of *operation* with any bodily movement. It is, as it were, the "assertion" of a bodily movement. The assertion of a sentence does not *cause* the sentence, obviously, since there is no separate event in which the assertion consists: you cannot execute an act of assertion, and then have the sentence come out: there is no assertion save *with* a sentence. And so with the doing of an action. There is no separate event of "doing" which then causes the bodily movement to happen. Rather, we cannot *just* do without doing *something*; "doing" is not something we can do all by itself. So, as with assertion, there is here no separate event which can stand to a bodily movement in the relationship of cause to effect. Actions cannot be "constant conjunctions" of inner doings and bodily movements. Rather, just as asserting a sentence is one complex event, and not the conjunction of two events, so the doing of an action is one complex event and not the conjunction of two events.

If we now think of volitions as standing to bodily movements in the same relation, more or less, in which the assertion of a sentence stands to the sentence asserted, might it not plausibly be argued that it is no objection that we cannot identify volitions as separate events? They are not separate events. We cannot *just* execute a volition, we can only execute a volitional action. Nor need we suppose that volitions *cause* actions, for on the one main theory of causation we have discussed, there is no separate event, consisting in a volition, which stands to a bodily movement in the relationship of cause to effect. Of course, the problem of analyzing complex events of the sort exemplified by assertions and of volitional actions becomes a central philosophical task, but at the least we should see that we already have room in our conceptual scheme for a concept of volition which is subject to none of the obvious criticisms. For we have the concept of assertion. And one might finally take the latter as a model for coping with Wittgenstein's question: if you substract *s* from the assertion of *s*, what would be left over?

47. In the light of these considerations, we might think once more of the quest for certainty which Descartes fathered upon philosophy. We might consider for a moment his celebrated proof of his own existence. He argued that since he thought, he existed; and the ringing sentence *cogito, ergo sum* has intrigued, and puzzled, philosophers ever since. They have been concerned especially with the exact nature of the *ergo*. Plainly, it does not logically follow from the sentence "I think" that "I exist." You cannot deduce "*m* exists" from "*m* thinks." To be sure, nobody can say of himself "I think but I do not exist"—but then nobody can say of himself "I do not exist" and expect that it could possibly be true if he in fact says it. It is a sentence which is made false through the fact that it is *said*. But this does not mean, when we say "I do not exist" cannot be true when uttered, that "I exist" is in some way a necessary truth in virtue of this. It is not a necessary truth; it does not involve a logical contradiction, even though its negate is not something which can both be said and be true in the mouth of him who says it. The latter is false through the assertion of it. But nothing quite like this happens when we replace the pronoun with the name of the individual who asserts the sentence. "Descartes exists" for example, is different from "I exist" as said by Descartes; and "Descartes does not exist," though false when Descartes says it, is not *made* false through the very assertion of it. Should Descartes have said "Descartes does not exist" we might have taken this as a piece of information, not knowing that the speaker was Descartes himself. But if he had said "I do not exist" that would be nonsense, no matter who the speaker was. And the reason, in part, is this. "Descartes exists" is a sentence, but "I exist" is not exactly a sentence. It is not true or false for the reason that "I" is a kind of variable. Compare this with $x + 7 = 12$. You cannot say whether this is true or false until a sentence is made out of it by replacing the variable with a constant; and it is true or false then depending upon what number we put for *x*. So with "I." It is a variable until it is *used* in an act of self-reference by a speaker. So when any sentence beginning with "I . . ." is used, the "I" refers to the speaker of it, and, with the act of reference completed this way, he to whom it refers exists. "I exist" becomes a sentence only when it is asserted. We know that whoever asserts it has to exist, and that "I do not exist" is belied by the completed act of reference which intelligible assertion presupposes. But then these considerations apply with any sentence in the first-person singular. Whenever such a string of words is asserted, there is a completed reference, and the existence of him to whom the pronoun refers is presupposed. It is presupposed by "I . . ." becoming a sentence. Most sentences are sentences whether asserted or not. They are not *made* sentences through the act of assertion. But when the subject is the first-person pronoun, we have something which only becomes a sentence when it is asserted. The act of assertion completes it and, when it is completed, it is automatically assured, through these facts, that he exists about whom the sentence is asserted, whether the sentence itself is true or false. It is in this manner that the *sum* comes from the *cogito*. It comes, not from the fact of cogitation but from the fact that *cogito* is asserted.

Descartes went on to say that he was a thinking thing—a *res cogitans*—on the grounds which we discussed in section 44, that he could not think of himself as not thinking: that this would be a self-defeating act. But the better argument would have been that he was an *agent*, a performer of actions. For the whole burden of his argument *cogito, ergo sum* derives not from the *content* or the *meaning* of *cogito*—"I think"—but, rather, from its *assertion*: *sum* would follow from whatever he asserted in virtue of his having asserted it. The fact that he had thoughts was less crucial than the fact that he did something with them: he *asserted* or *denied* them, and was insofar an agent. It is a characteristic of Descartes's arguments that their conclusions follow not so much from the content of what he may be saying but from the actions involved in saying them. And the metaphysical question which his writings leave us is this: what must be the case in order that there be agents, assertions counting, after all, as actions with sentences, and

Descartes having proved that he was an agent in this sense. This returns us to the topic of action.

48. The issue is to what degree Descartes, as an agent, has restricted that special class of sentences which consists in *assertions*. Why, in view of the analogy between sentences and bodily movements, as between assertions and volitions, would he not equally and in the same sense be an agent when he moves his arm? The concept of action, as we saw, cuts across the distinction, however it may be phrased, between the mental and the physical. I may act bodily, or I may act mentally. Might we not think, that as an assertion is not two things (a sentence and an operation with it) but one complex whole, and as an action is not two distinct things (a movement, say, and an operation with it) but one complex thing, so an agent is not two distinct things (an agent and a body) but one complex whole: a *person*? Descartes's proof, after all, has to be not that he is a *res cogitans*, but a *res agens*, an *acting* thing. Then he is related to whatever it is that he may perform actions with—whether his mind or his body or both—in a different way than the way in which his mind and body would be related. He is not to be identified with his mind, any more than he is to be identified with his body, since an agent need not as such be, or have, some mental state. If this curious line of thought is followed out, the mind-body problem becomes metaphysically less pressing than the agent-instrument problem, if we may put it so. Descartes himself, in his final *Meditation*, hinted to as much: "I am not [merely] in my body as a pilot is in a ship," he writes there. I do not, he means to say, move my arm the way a pilot moves a rudder, by turning some internal wheel and activating some covert mechanism. No: I move it directly. And should someone find it puzzling that we should do such things, we might ask how he activated whatever interior thing he feels the activation of which to be required in explanation of how our arm moves. Does he not do *that* directly? And if it is not puzzling that he should do so, why should it be puzzling that we can do so with our arms? Or, if he feels we need an interior episode, why does he not need one there? If he does, of course, there is an infinite regression to have to face. And action is impossible. If there are any actions at all, there have to be these *basic acts* (as I term them), acts we do without first doing something else. So I am not separated from my body in a way which would require that some event in me be required to cause the movement of my body. Rather, the connection is very close and non-causal. But if this is so, it seems plausible to suppose ourselves to be just the sorts of complex entities our analysis has suggested that we are. We are not minds in bodies, nor embodied minds, but agents with, as it happens, bodies.

If there is anything to these considerations, actions, though complex, are primitive sorts of events, as agents, though complex again, are primitive sorts of entities, to be listed as such in the inventory of the furniture of the world. If minds are separate from bodies, which we have no good reason to believe they are, then there might be agents with just minds and no bodies, which is, as it happens, just the view of things which Descartes attained to in the early *Meditations* when he set out to ask whether, outside himself, or, in his idiom, whether, outside his ideas and himself, there was anything at all. But even in this reduced universe, there would not only be minds, there would be *agents*. Such an ontology was in fact endorsed by Bishop Berkeley, for whom there were two sorts of entities in the universe, spirits and ideas. Spirits *had* ideas, but were not congruent with the ideas they had and, indeed, Berkeley argued, spirits could achieve no idea of themselves. It is this, of course, which Descartes meant to diminish in importance when he argued that abstract as his idea of his self was, our ideas of things are hardly less abstract when we analyze them. Berkeley, whom we recall as wanting to argue that things are only ideas, must be understood as saying that spirits are not things—a conception we can appreciate now by saying that agents are not bodies, but *have* bodies, and are not to be identified with the bodies that they have (though they have no separate existence). Berkeley also held that spirits are free. If we mean by agents what he meant by spirits, so are agents free. But by contrast, bodies are not. And the problem now becomes vexed indeed as to how agents should be free though their bodies should be, as we say, determined. This brings us to the problem, or cluster of problems, which to the layman is perhaps regarded as the paradigm philosophical problem, namely, the problem of free will.

This is held to be a problem of some importance, for our status as free agents, it is said, is presupposed by the ascription of moral predicates to us, in the respect that, if we are not in the required sense free, then we, no more than sticks or stones, are subjects of moral predication. I believe, despite a great deal of subtle argument to the contrary, that this is a correct consequence, and I should like, if only briefly, to produce an argument intended to show that freedom and determinism really are incompatible teachings, and that, if we are not free, then, for at least one crucial class of moral predicates, we are not subjects of moral predication. After that, we can attempt to pick up some of the pieces which this curious metaphysic leaves shattered upon the ground, and see whether we can get a coherent picture of agents, who are free, being inseparable from but complexly related to bodies (or minds, for that matter), which are determined.

49. By determinism I shall mean the theory that whatever happens is causally necessitated to happen, to the exclusion of any other thing. Other forms or versions of determinism are doubtless defensible, but only this one, I think, is of direct philosophical pertinence to the famous free will problem. It alone seems quite unequivocally to rule out that, under those very conditions which a determinist would regard as determining a happening e, any happening other than e could have happened instead. For suppose that under a set of conditions C, either e or f *could* happen, and e *does* happen. Then either no explanation can be given of why e rather than f took place, or else the set of conditions must be supplemented in some way, so that we may now explain why f did not happen and e did. But, since only the latter alternative seems compatible with determinism, determinism seems committed to the view that, for whatever happens, there are conditions under which it and nothing other than it could happen, and hence that whatever happens *has* to *happen*, given the conditions which hold.

It is this, I believe, which would have to be denied by any anti-determinist, whether he *also* happened to believe in free will, the latter being but a species of anti-determinism. All anti-determinists must hold that *sometimes* at least, something other than what happens could happen instead under the identical conditions, in the precise sense of 'could happen instead' from which it follows that what happened did not *have* to happen, in the determinist's sense of 'have to happen.' There may be other senses or uses of 'could happen instead' which would not entail the denial of determinism, but I cannot suppose reference to them would do other than postpone or evade the issue. Thus both determinists and their opponents might agree that one may without self-contradiction deny 'Under *C, e* has to happen.' Since this sentence might *logically* be denied, and its denial might *logically* be possible, 'Under *C, f* happened instead of *e*' could *logically* have been true. But this sense of logical possibility is utterly irrelevant to a dispute concerning how the world *is*, and so has not the slightest interest for the contest between determinists and their opponents.

If some happenings are actions performed by men, then the determinist is of course committed to the view that these, too, are necessitated to happen, to the exclusion of any other thing. Free-willism, I should think, is required to suppose that there are actions, and that, under the identical conditions *C*, a man *m* could have acted other than he *did* act. So even if determinism were proved false, and anti-determinism were proved correct, it would not *follow* that free-willism were correct. Thus, under *C*, a man *m* does action *a* and something else could have happened under *C* without it following that *m* could have performed another *action* than the one he in fact performed. Or, for that matter, there might be no such things as action, so that even if anti-determinism were right, free-willism would not be.

It is accordingly not enough, as William James once suggested, that free-willists demolish determinism. They must in addition demonstrate that *their* form of anti-determinism is correct. But since free-willism is the view that under identical conditions, men could act differently than they *do* act, it follows that something other than what happens could, under the identical conditions, have happened instead. So free-willism entails anti-determinism, and hence entails that determinism is false. Free-willism and determinism could both be false but not both be true. To that extent they are incompatible even if anti-determinism and anti-free-willism are compatible and might, indeed, come to just the same thing. It would do the free-willist no good whatever if some events were not necessitated unless these should also happen to be human acts.

I do not believe that it follows from the mere concept of an action that, if men perform actions, it *must* be true that they always, under the identical conditions, could have acted other than they did. For there may be actions which men *cannot help performing* under some conditions, so that, under those conditions, they are impotent to do otherwise. I shall term these *compulsive* actions. They are illustrated perhaps, by the drinking of an alcoholic who has not the power to do otherwise, who suffers from what the ancients termed weakness of the will.

On the other hand, it would be a travesty of determinism to suggest that every action is a compulsive one. Hence it must presumably be compatible with determinism that sometimes, when men perform actions, they are not impotent to perform them, and so have the power to do otherwise; and so, finally, something other than what did happen *could* have happened instead. But this must be a sense of 'could have happened instead' which is irrelevant to the issue, and I mention it because it gives to the thesis that '*m* has it in his power to do otherwise', a sense which is compatible with the claim of determinism that *m* is necessitated to act as he does, given the conditions which hold. If free-willism were understood as the thesis that, except for compulsive actions, men have it always in their power to act other than as they do, free-willism *would* be compatible with determinism.

In allowing this power to men, however, the determinist must insist that they have not the power to exercise it, since they are necessitated to act as they do. And we must, accordingly, now characterize free-willism as the theory that sometimes, under identical conditions, men can act other than as they do, not merely in the sense that they are not impotent to act other than as they do, but that they have the power to exercise their power to do otherwise. This, then, restores the incompatibility. If free-willism is true, then, when men act under a set of conditions, it is some-times true that *nothing is lacking* for them to act otherwise. When they so act, theirs is a free act.

Now it seems to me that there is a class of actions which, if they occur at all, *must* be free acts. These are what I term *forebear-ances*. When a man forebears doing *a*, it follows that he does not do *a*; but there are, of course, many ways in which '*m* does not do *a*' could be true without it also being true that *m* forebears doing *a*. The mere observation, accordingly, that *m* happens not to be doing *a* (and there are so many things we are not doing at any given moment that it is difficult to see why this observation should be ordinarily made at all), does not entail that our not doing *a* is an action of ours. Yet we surely recognize a difference between cases where, as a matter of fact, I am not raising my arm, and cases where my not raising my arm is an action on my part, e.g., where I deliberately disobey the command to *raise* it. There my not raising my arm may be the most important fact about me at the time. To be sure, it can sometimes be that I am *not* doing some-thing, and my doing that thing *is* an action of mine, but I am none-theless not *forebearing*. The classical example of this is perhaps Ulysses who, knowing in advance that neither he nor any man can forebear responding to the Sirens' call, has himself bound to the mast so that he *will not* respond to the Sirens' call. His *not* re-sponding is the deliberate action he performed, but he did not forebear, and perhaps could not. The distinction between not doing *a* and doing *not-a* is extremely important in moral and legal dis-course, and is closely connected with the topics of temperance and self-control, of withstanding impulse and temptation, with which the ancient moralists were so much occupied.

A determinist may wish to reject the distinction, but we must point out that an exactly analogous one holds in the concept of causality. There we distinguish between one event not causing *e* —which is causal inoperacy—and another event causing *not-e*— which is an instance of causation, namely, a prevention. So doing *not-a* is an action, just as causing *not-e* is a cause.

An important logical feature of the concept of forebearance is this. If a man cannot perform an action, then neither can he forebear performing that action. A dumb man does not *forebear* speaking: unable to speak, his silence is not a virtue, for it is never an action. An impotent man does not *forebear* womanizing: incapable of sexuality, his abstinence is not a virtue and never an action. An unmarried woman cannot *forebear* adultery. An unarmed man cannot *forebear* shooting his neighbor. The totally impecunious cannot *forebear* wasting money. Chastity, thrift, clemency— all the virtues—consist in doing *not-a*, that is forebearing *a*, and this in every instance logically presupposes that whoever is virtuous can do otherwise. But now if *so much as a single condition necessary* for the occurrence of an event is lacking, that event cannot take place. So if a *single condition* for *m* doing *a* is lacking, *m* cannot do *a*. By definition, if *m* lacks the power to exercise the power to do *a*, one condition, and indeed the very condition insisted upon by the determinist, is lacking for him to do *a*. So he cannot do *a*. So neither can he forebear doing *a*. Hence, if he ever forebears *a*, every condition necessary for him to do *a* must hold, *including* his having the power to exercise the power to do *a*. Forebearances, then, would be free acts, and if there are forebearances, determinism is false.

There may, of course, be no forebearances. It follows, then, that there would be no virtues, nor would anyone ever be temperate. This would seem to fly in the face of facts. I do not here insist, however, that we forebear. My concern only has been to show that free will and determinism are incompatible and incidentally to suggest the way in which mortality—or at least the theory of virtues— presupposes the truth of free-willism and the falsity of determinism as I have characterized them.

50. We may pause here to remark again that it is not ever in the interests of philosophy to deny any facts. When, as in such singular cases as the paradoxes of Zeno, there appears to be a radical discrepancy between a theory and some set of plain facts, it is tempting but in the end unacceptable to drum the facts out of the universe. The word "real" has often been used with the reckless abandon of one of the pasteboard duchesses in *Alice in Wonderland* to dismiss from consideration something which, for whatever reason, has no place in or is even incompatible with a favored thesis. In the present instance, there is no better guideline to sanity than to hold on to the fact we have established in the various sciences which have to do with human existence. There are plain and undeniable facts having to do with the causation of human choices, established on the part of social psychology, of economics, of sociology, and anthropology. It is undeniable that much of our behavior can be explained, can even be exhibited as lawlike, that we all are products of our time and place and our class location; that our physiological and sexual cast deeply determines our chances at happiness and limits in some cases totally the choices that we may exercise. But none of this, in the end, counts any more as evidence for the metaphysical denial of the freedom of the will than does the fact that we sometimes make mistakes count in establishment of a thesis of general skepticism. Determinism, again, must doubtless be regarded a scientific ideal, in that science cannot ultimately suppose that any event or set of events is in principle recalcitrant to explanation. Indeed, as we have seen in our earlier glimpse of Kant, it may plausibly be proposed that causation is something we are constrained to apply to any experience whatever, so that nothing could intelligibly be counted experience which failed to conform to the structure of universal causation. But if our argument of the last section is correct, if determinism is true, there are and can be no actions, in the sense which seems required by the thesis of free will. So the question then is whether philosophical determinism is in fact true.

Let us, however, remind ourselves of some considerations which emerged in our protracted analogy between assertions and actions, and hence between sentences and bodily movements. Sentences, just as such, are physical things, bits of ink on paper, or bundles of waves in the air. As physical events, they are what they are, and subject to all the same laws of chemistry and acoustics. These are concerned not at all with whether these sentences are true or false. The acoustics of false sentences cannot differ from the acoustic of true ones. Basic science is indifferent to such a distinction. Again, arm movements are just as they are, whether they are actions or not, whether they are "done" or not: the physiology of motion is just the same, whether there are actions or not. And again, the web of events is just as it is, whether what we do succeeds or not. A stone hits or misses a target, but we have no need for a different physics of projectile motion for successes than for failures. Physics is neutral to such distinctions. So far as science need be concerned, there are no actions; there are no distinctions between those events which are actions, and those which are not. If this is so, then free-willism is not at least incompatible with science, since science is merely neutral with regard to it. If this is so, no fact for or against free-willism may be found in the sciences, nor in the structure of the theories which science employs. And this means that no examination of the world from the perspective of science will reveal a distinction which will tell for or against either side in this controversy.

Such a claim, as it happens, was exactly favored by Kant. The world of phenomena, the experienced world, was causal through and through, inasmuch as the general principle of causality was implicated in the very conception of experience as intelligible. But this means, roughly as we have argued, that no experience could count either in favor or disfavor of the free will or anti-free will controversy. No experience, since experience perforce is going to be causally structured. But this only means that the distinction between actions and mere events is not a distinction we can observe. Which, to revert to our example, is like saying that no experience merely of a sentence will tell us whether the sentence itself is true or false. Language is of a piece, whether true or false, and experience is of a piece, whether it contains actions or not. And so, too, with the curious ontology of Berkeley cited above. Ideas (= things) all can be subject to universal determinism, without spirits being so, since spirits are not things (= ideas). The distinction between spirits and things is not a distinction experience can reveal, since experience is, after all, of things. It is a distinction at right angles, so to speak, to experience; or at right angles to the world so far as the world is what we experience. And this suggests that the relation of ourselves to what we experience is not a further element in what we experience, not a further fact in the world. The connection between ourselves and the world is not a fact internal to the world itself. And with this we may begin to make a connection with what we earlier offered in characterization of philosophy itself, and its relation to science.

51. Let us consider for a moment what we mean by truth, or at least what we mean when we say, of a sentence, that the sentence is true. Certainly, its being true is not one of its *properties* in the way in which its being grammatical is one of its properties, or in the way in which it has seven words or twenty sounds. Its being true cannot be one of the structural properties of a sentence for the simple reason that it has to be just the very same sentence which is either true or false, as the case may be, and if true and false sentences were structurally different, we should be able to read from their surfaces whether they were true or false. We would be able to say: that sentence cannot be false, that one cannot be true, for they have different properties. In recent times, some very radical philosophers have proposed that truth is in *no sense whatever* a property of sentences. When we say that *s* is true, they have argued, we are not ascribing a property to *s*, but rather are expressing *agreement* with *s* or conceding that *s*, or some such thing; "is true" is not, according to them, so much a descriptive expression as it is the performance of a verbal act. And in proposing this, they have taken a stand against a famous and important theory of truth, known as the semantical theory of truth, propounded by the logician Alfred Tarski. Since Tarski's theory is somewhat relevant to our concerns, we had better say a few words in explanation of it.

It is difficult in the present context to cite the rather impressive set of considerations which go to support the semantical theory of truth, for many of these are technical and refined. But perhaps the most serious contribution that theory makes is the manner in which it prevents certain paradoxes from arising. The relevant paradoxes—the so-called semantical paradoxes—are exemplified in the celebrated paradox of Epimenides the Cretan, who asserted that all Cretans are liars. If what he said is true, then *he*, though a Cretan, has not lied, since lies are false. But then if it *is* true that Cretans all are liars, what he said is false. Obviously, "All

Cretans are liars" could be true: it merely could not be true when said by any Cretan, for, when said by him, it is false if it is true, and true if it is false. And this is not a pleasant anomaly. But obviously the difficulty does not so much lie with the sentence itself, as with the circumstances of its utterance: it simply cannot be unparadoxically uttered by Cretans. We cannot but detect here features already remarked in our discussion of the *cogito* of Descartes, where the circumstances of utterance underwrite, as it were, the truth or falsity of the sentence which otherwise is unexceptionable.

Now one consideration emerges from this with a clarity which it is easy to see in retrospect, but not terribly easy to see with the unaided logical eye: it is that Epimenides' sentence refers to *itself* in his mouth—being something that a Cretan has said—whereas it does not refer to itself when said, say, by me (who am not a Cretan). Now if we can manage to inhibit self-reference, we stop such paradoxes from arising. And one way of doing this is to tighten a distinction between *using* a sentence and *mentioning* a sentence. Thus, when I should say "The last sentence said by Plato is true," the expression "The last sentence said by Plato" *mentions* a sentence, a sentence no doubt in Greek and in any event not a sentence known by me. But suppose I did know it. Suppose the last sentence uttered by Plato was "All things are Good." Now I could say "All things are Good is true." But "All things are Good," quite as much as "The last sentence uttered by Plato," mentions a sentence. But while this is obvious in the one case, it is less obvious in the other, where that which I employ to mention the sentence *has the same shape and the same design as the sentence which it mentions*! It is then difficult to notice that, in the one case, we are dealing with a sentence and in the other case with an expression which is the name of a sentence, or which, at least, mentions a sentence. Now if we think of such contexts as ". . . is true," what we can fit into the slot is not a sentence but, rather, the *name* of a sentence. So in "*s* is true" we do not *use s* as a sentence: we use *s* as a *name* for a sentence. "The sky is blue" then merely mentions the sentence "The sky is blue" when it appears in the sentence "The sky is blue is true." In the latter context, the expression does not refer to itself, any more than a name refers to itself: a name refers to whatever it is the name of. One may see this in such cases as "Arthur is my name." In this context, "Arthur" does not function as my name but as the *name* of my name! And once we have opened up a distance between sentences and names of sentences, the possibilities of self-reference are blocked: *s* does not refer to *itself* in the context "*s* is true." It refers to whatever sentence it may happen to mention. And about *that* sentence, it says: it is true.

52. But having said as much, the question remains as to what sort of property it is we are ascribing to *s* when we say that *s* is true. And here the answer is not simple to give. Tarski was content to say that so long as it was recognized that "is true" ascribes a property to sentences, it would not especially matter to him what sort of property it was. He regarded his theory compatible with any theory of truth whatever: his was not so much a theory of truth as it was a theory of "is true." And it is, of course, this which the philosophers referred to above have contested is not a *correct* theory. They have wanted to say that it is not the *use* of the words "is true" to ascribe a property to sentences, but rather, it is their *use* to express agreement, or some such thing. And what is especially interesting with this thesis is that, if we can have *shown* that the use of "is true" is never really descriptive at all, then we need not especially have a theory of *truth* at all. Indeed, it would have been an error on the part of philosophers to suppose that a theory of truth were required at all, and this error would have been due to misreading "is true" as a descriptive predicate when it is not that at all.

It is this latter bold suggestion, rather than the particular detail of their treatment, which makes this appeal to linguistic usage of philosophical interest. For after all, philosophers have asked for millennia about the nature of truth: and how convenient it would be if it could be shown that their entire quest was the consequence of having misrepresented the linguistic force of a certain phrase! This deflationist attempt to reduce questions of truth to questions of "true," and to thwart the enterprise of seeking theories of truth, is due to the British philosopher P. F. Strawson. It is but one of a class of such theories which, as a class, have attracted a high degree of philosophical interest over the past few years. These theories are dissolutive in character, and their criterion is essentially this: that they propose to show that certain questions, which seem to require and at the same time to resist philosophical answers, have arisen from a failure to recognize what is the correct *use* of language in connection with seemingly puzzling expressions. When the use has been made clear, the propensity to pose the question should subside. Thus, when we recognize that "That's true" does not say anything about whatever sentence it is which "That" may refer to, but rather (merely) expresses the speaker's agreement, the seemingly deep question "What is truth" ought no longer to be deemed a genuine question.

The paradigm dissolutive theory is, perhaps, the emotivist theory of moral language, according to which such sentences as "*a* is good"—or any sentence which uses a typical term of the moral vocabulary, viz., "right," "wrong," "bad,"—does not assert any *fact* about *a*, and does not state something which is true or false in the way in which "*a* is round" is true or false. It rather evinces the speakers attitude towards *a*: in saying "*a* is good" I am not using language descriptively but expressively. And the strategy of this analysis is plain. If "*a* is good" is not descriptive but expressive, no effort need be made to determine in what goodness (objectively) consists, nor what "good" (objectively) means. Objectively, it means nothing, according to this theory; descriptively, it is *meaningless*. Hence the entire vast sequence of philosophical attempts to define or discover the nature of the Good have been misguided efforts, which would have been due to the unhappy inference that since the sentences which use ethical terms are grammatically of a piece with the ordinary descriptive sentence, they must be true or false in the ordinary way. There is no *un*ordinary way in which a sentence may be true or false, and *these* sentences, had they been properly seen as *expressive*, could not have been seen as perhaps stating some deep and inaccessible fact. As with Strawson's account of "is true," this is a bold account hoping, at one stroke, to wash away all the *philosophical* problems of ethics. It is ironic that the old quests for the True, the Good, and the Beautiful should have given way to analyses of "true," "good," and "beautiful" which, if they are correct, make the question of what these terms may denote uninteresting. Who could be seriously interested in "true," "good," and "beautiful" if their sole function is to express feelings and attitudes! It would be like being interested in "OK," "Three cheers," and "Zowie."

Doubtless, these redirective, deflationist analyses would be silenced once and for all if it could be shown that there were objective correlates for these serious sounding words. But in view of the dismally long, and singularly unproductive investigations into the "nature" of truth, goodness, and the like, and in view of the fact that we appear to use these critical words spontaneously, with an ease utterly disproportionate to the alleged difficulty in determining what goodness, say, consists in—in view of these things, there is something refreshing in the brash suggestion that the words only express feelings pro and con.

Of course, they may not express feelings. They may have some different sort of use altogether. But the important thing to have discovered would have been that the words are not descriptive, or not primarily descriptive. If that could have been shown, the precise characterization of their use would be by contrast merely a question of detail: and not even of very considerable philosophical interest. That "good" should be used in English, for example, to commend rather than to express attitudes and feelings, belongs to the sociolinguistic study of our language, and not to philosophy at all. And indeed, if it could be shown that the meanings of sentences is their use, the analysis of sentences would now be the province of the sociology of linguistic practice, and philosophy would be finished; it would have become an empirical science of only limited theoretical interest. To be sure, philosophers like Wittgenstein and Austin often behaved as though the end of philosophy were in sight, as though we were in the last phases of a long wandering in a linguistic wilderness, the promised land of the empirical science of correct usage lying before us; a banal paradise, perhaps, but to be preferred, after all, to the protraction of a state of illusion. Perhaps reality is not at all what we should like it to be, but the mature cannot will the perduring of illusion, and surely not the philosopher, who has prided himself for millennia as a seeker after reality! The dissipation of a dream is a bitter, thankless task, one which arouses a very natural resentment; but what choice, the linguistic philosopher must ask, do we have any longer?

53. I do not believe the matter rests here, or that philosophy is after all, either over or transformed. And perhaps we might turn again to the concept of truth. Let it be agreed that "*s* is true," in case it should be descriptive, does not ascribe to the sentence *s* some structural feature. For reasons by now perhaps painfully clear, truth, if a property of sentences, cannot be that sort of property. It must, if a property, be one which a sentence may gain or lose while remaining just the same sentence; it cannot, as it were, be an essential property of a sentence that it should be true. And one way in which this might be feasible would be if the truth of a sentence were like a *value*—and falsity another value—in the respect that a sentence might sustain a change in value without being a different sentence. Now some things, when they change internally, change in value accordingly. As an apple, for example, loses its freshness, its value decreases. As a building deteriorates, so does its value. And many cases similar to this can be found, where changes in value are sometimes a function of internal changes in the thing itself. There are other cases where something may change in value without any internal change. A copy of a book may increase in value through the gradual loss of all other copies; its uniqueness confers upon it a certain value, though uniqueness is not an internal trait of a copy of a book. Scarcity, in other words, is an example in which the value which something bears is externally determined. Surely, if truth and falsity are values, they must be determined externally. For sentences are not true or false just as *such*. Sentences are *made* true, or *made* false only when asserted. It is not the assertions which make them true or false (except in some rather rare cases): it is rather that asserting a sentence puts it in position to be made true or false. The very same sentence, when asserted, is either true or false, depending upon . . . what? What makes the difference?

It is very natural to say that change in the value of a sentence, or better, change in the truth value of a sentence, is a uniquely determined function of *changes in the world*. Thus, the sentence "The sky is blue" may be taken as undergoing changes in truth value exactly as a function of changes in the color of the sky: as the sky goes from blue to grey, the sentence goes from true to false. It is through a relation between that sentence and the world that the sentence becomes true or becomes false. Assertion is an action which, as it were, engages language with the world. But assertion is less important than our discussion suggests. For we may say, of a given sentence, that were someone to assert it, he would say something true, or something false, because the required relationship between that sentence and the world holds, or fails to hold.

I shall speak of this relationship as *correspondence*. To understand a sentence, which is descriptive, is to know to what the sentence is to correspond when it is true. In this regard, one cannot understand such sentences without knowing how the world must be if they are true. And this means: to understand such a sentence is to be able to tell when the relationship of correspondence is satisfied. This does not entail that we cannot understand false sentences. For the difference between truth and falsity is wholly external. We understand a good deal more than we *know*. Understanding leaves undetermined what truth value a sentence *in fact* bears, even if we could not be said to understand it if we were unable to tell what it would be like in the world if the sentence itself were true.

Correspondence is a very weak relation. There need be, and probably very seldom is, no deep congruity of form between the sentence and what makes it true. It is because philosophers have at times demanded some such *strong* criterion of resemblance, or isomorphism, between sentence and world that the correspondence theory of truth has seemed wrong or impossible. But I ask nothing so dramatic of the relationship of correspondence.

Notice, however, what follows from our theory. Truth is not a property of the world. It is not a property of sentences either. To look at the world in the hope of unearthing truth is as misguided as to peer at sentences in the vagrant hope of hitting upon some internal structural feature in which truth consists. Truth belongs neither to language nor to the world, but to the relationship between them. A sentence is true when it corresponds with the world, as something is real when it corresponds with a sentence. Words like "true" and "real" then describe nothing in the world. Nor do they describe features of sentences. They pertain wholly to the space which opens up between the world and language. And since I long since declared that philosophers are concerned with the space between language and the world, it is not to be wondered that the analysis of truth is a paradigmatic philosophical problem!

The linguists are right. Philosophers would have been misled in looking into the dark corners of the world for some evasive, important entity called Truth. They were right, too, in saying that truth is not a property of sentences. They are even right in saying that "*s* is true" does not say something about *s*. They only are wrong in saying that "*s* is true" is not descriptive, and even there they are not wholly wrong. It describes neither the world nor *s*. It says only that a certain relationship between the world and *s* is satisfied. But this is not a further description of the world nor a further characterization of *s*.

54. Having now worked through a paradigmatic philosophical problem, let us consider a little further, before we conclude, the character of the philosophical subject matter. A theory of truth tells us under what conditions statements about the world are true without itself being a statement about the world. A theory of knowledge tells us under what conditions we have knowledge of the world without itself being a further piece of knowledge of the world. Thus men may know, concerning the world, everything they know without their knowledge of the world being extended by the further knowledge of what *knowledge* is! Much the same considerations apply to their possession of truths. Men could possess whatever truths they do possess, without themselves possessing a theory of truth. A theory of truth does not augment the stock of truths, any more than a theory of knowledge increases the scope of what we know. Philosophy, in providing theories of truth or theories of knowledge then adds nothing to the body of truths we possess or knowledge which we have. Only science, broadly construed, of course, does this. Philosophy only analyzes what it is for a sentence to be true, or what it is for a man to have knowledge.

You may call this increment of understanding a further piece of truth or a further bit of knowledge if you wish to, but you pay a price. Knowledge, in the primary sense of the concept, is of the world. To know that s is to know that the world is the way that s says that it is. To know that this is so is not, after all, to know a further fact regarding the *world*. It is, rather, to know something about a relationship between the world and s, or better, between the world and him who knows s. Of course, one may say that s, as a sentenial thing, is in the world. So, for the matter, is he in the world who knows s. After all, are we not in the world? Is not the relationship between knowers and the world the relationship of being contained in it?

The answer is yes and no. As men, we are in the world, as clouds are and clods, as fish and birds and the stars. But as knowers, our relation to the world is different from this. However we may be in the world, to have *knowledge* is to be, as it were, outside the world: for the world is what we have knowledge of, and between us and the world there is then a relationship which is not a relationship internal to the world itself. There is, for the matter, a relationship of this sort between ourselves and ourselves, when it is we, ourselves, of which we should have knowledge. As an existentialist might like to say, as knowers, our way of *being in the world* is not to be in it, to be related to the world externally rather than internally. To analyze these relations then is the whole task of philosophy. And that is why, because it is concerned with the relations between the world and ourselves, it would not be right to say: philosophy tells us about the world. And hence, in the primary sense of the matter, it would be wrong to say: philosophy gives us knowledge of the world. And that is the difference between philosophy and science.

The world, we might say, contains conscious entities, including ourselves, and the conditions under which consciousness is possible is an important factual question. But to be conscious of the world (or of ourselves, as part of the world) is to have the world as an *object*, external to oneself (or oneself as an object, external to oneself). There are, then, two ways of being related to the world: and one of these is the province of science, and the other is the province of philosophy. And this duality of ways of being related to the world is irreducible and unavoidable for creatures such as ourselves. In every way in which science wants to insist, we are in the world. And yet, because we are what we are, between the world and ourselves there is always a distance.

55. This can be put in another way. We are, in one respect, related to the world in the sense of being contained in it, as further items in the inventory. But there is another respect in which, curious as it may sound, the world is contained in *us*. This is the way, for example, in which what we are conscious of is contained in the consciousness of it, *as* the object of consciousness. Or in the way in which the assertion of a sentence contains the sentence. Or in the way in which an action contains a bodily movement. There are other cases. Think, for a moment, of a statue. It is in the world as so much bronze or marble. Located in the physical order of the world, or in the social order of the world, for that matter, it is subject to all the causes and forces science requires us to recognize. It is contained in the world in that way, but in another way, it contains the world, or part of it. For the work of art contains, as it were, its matter: its bronze or marble. This is a tenuous thing, of course. It is not as though were one to subtract the bronze or marble one would have left the art work in its purity. This would be like hoping to subtract the sentence from an assertion, or the bodily movement from an act, and hope to have something pure left over. Or, for the matter, to subtract the object of consciousness from consciousness itself in the hope of having consciousness unadulterated. Without a world, there is no consciousness; without bodies, there are no acts; without sentences, there are no assertions; without bronze and marble (or plastic or wood) there are no art works. But it does not follow that the art work is only the bronze, the action only the arm movement, the assertion only the sentence, or the consciousness only the world. Without the world, there

would be nothing: the world is all there is. Yet, if actions are complex events, as we have suggested, why should not the world in just that way in which it contains (and is contained by) agents be complex too? If it contained no agents, no knowers, no consciousness, it would of course contain neither art nor philosophy. The world would be what it is, but it would never be an *object* for itself. It becomes an object only when a distance opens up between it and parts of itself. Science describes the world as though there were no gap of this sort, though, of course, the very existence of this gap is what makes science possible. Science exhibits, hopefully, the structure of the world. Art, in its way, reveals the world in the respect that, between the work of art and the world, there has to be a gap or distance of just the sort which exists between language and the world, or between science and the world. There are many such gaps. Only between philosophy and the world are there none; not because philosophy is closer to the world than these other spiritual activities, but only because philosophy is concerned with these gaps and not intrinsically with what is on either side of them.

But in revealing these gaps between the world and parts of itself, the world is revealed by philosophy to have a complexity we could not have suspected from these other spiritual activities alone, though it would remain just the world it is without philosophy, swept by just the same causal forces which determine it, whether it is spiritualized or not.

Collateral Reading

There is an important respect in which all philosophers, despite the radically diverse historical conditions under which they wrote and thought, are intellectual contemporaries. Philosophers today are often as much concerned with arguments and analyses and theories of Plato and of Aristotle as they are with those of their strict contemporaries. All intellectual disciplines have a history, but almost uniquely in philosophy is its history self-consciously carried in the minds of its practitioners as part of their intellectual equipment. It is tacitly conceded that one must be on speaking terms with the masters in order to say anything significant oneself. There are no philosophical primitives.

The following works are drawn from present and past indifferently. They are listed here because I have chiefly had them in mind when writing one or another section of this book, and the sections to which they are especially relevant are cited in brackets. Hence this is a highly selective bibliography, with no pretense to completeness of any sort. From the conspicuous number of citations, it must be obvious that the *Meditations* of Descartes has raised the dominating issues of the volume. This is only natural, inasmuch as it is upon a Cartesian framework that philosophy since his time has been arrayed. But I have perhaps brooded over Descartes's work more than I have that of any other thinker, and in introducing students to philosophy, the *Meditations* has always been my chosen text.

I make no effort here to cite special editions, or to locate a piece of writing except where it is not part of the standard corpus.

Austin, J. L. "Other Minds." Frequently reprinted, but perhaps most conveniently available in Austin's *Philosophical Papers*. (Oxford, 1961) [9, 52].

Ayer, A. J. *Language, Truth, and Logic* [4, 9, 26, 28, 52].

Berkeley, George. *Principles of Human Knowledge* [11, 20, 21, 22, 34, 48, 50].

Carnap, Rudolph. *Meaning and Necessity* [12].

Carnap, Rudolph. "Testability and Meaning." Anthologized in Feigl, H., and M. Brodbeck (eds.). *Readings in the Philosophy of Science*. (New York, 1953) [26].

Danto, A. *Analytical Philosophy of Knowledge*. (Cambridge, 1968) [31, 53].

Danto, A. "Basic Actions." *American Philosophical Quarterly*, II, 2 [40, 47, 48].

Danto, A. "Freedom and Forebearance." In Lehrer, K. (ed.). *Freedom and Determinism*. (New York, 1966) [49].

Descartes, R. *Meditations* [9, 17, 20, 21, 22, 23, 34, 35, 40, 47, 48].

Frege, Gottlob. "On Sense and Reference." In Geach, P., and M. Black (eds.) *Translations from the Philosophical Writings of Gottlob Frege* [12, 43].

Hare, R. M. *The Language of Morals* [9, 52].

Hempel, C. G. *Fundamentals of Concept Formation in the Empirical Sciences*. (Chicago, 1952) [13, 26].

Hume, David. *Enquiry Concerning Human Understanding* [11, 20, 29, 34, 41].

James, William. *Pragmatism* [4].

James, William. "The Will To Believe" [4].

James, William. "Does Consciousness Exist?" [38].

Kant, Immanuel. *Critique of Pure Reason* [19, 42, 50].

Kant, Immanuel. *Prolegomena to any Future Metaphysics* [14, 15, 16, 29].

Locke, John. *An Essay Concerning Human Understanding* [11, 20, 21, 36].

Mill, J. S. *A System of Logic* [12, 15, 27].

Moore, G. E. *Principia Ethica* [10].

Nietzsche, F. *Beyond Good and Evil* [29, 34].

Peirce, C. S. "How to Make our Ideas Clear" [4, 19].

Popper, Karl. *The Logic of Scientific Discovery* [28].

Quine, W. V. O. "Two Dogmas of Empiricism." Reprinted in his *From a Logical Point of View*. (Cambridge, Mass., 1953) [11, 13, 14].

Ryle, Gilbert. *The Concept of Mind* [44, 45, 46].

St. Anselm. *Proslogion*. Traditionally relevant portions of this, together with comments by other philosophers on the ontological argument, may be found in a paperback edited by Alvin Plantinga. *The Ontological Argument*. (New York, 1965) [19].

Smart, J. J. C. "Sensations and Brain Processes." *Philosophical Review*, LXVIII [43, 44, 45].

Spinoza, B. *Ethics* [38].

Strawson, P. F. *Individuals* [44].

Strawson, P. F. "Truth." Conveniently available, along with other useful discussions, in George Pitcher (ed.). *Truth.* (New York, 1964) [9, 51, 52].

Tarski, Alfred. "The Semantic Conception of Truth." Reprinted in Feigl, H., and W. Sellars (eds.). *Readings in Philosophical Analysis.* (New York, 1949) [51].

Wittgenstein, L. *Philosophical Investigations* [4, 9, 26, 28, 52].

Wittgenstein, L. *Tractatus Logico-Philosophicus* [14].

Good and up-to-date bibliographies on most philosophical topics may be found appended to the articles on these in Paul Edwards (ed.), *The Encyclopedia of Philosophy* (New York: Free-Press, 1967), 8 volumes.

72 73   12 11 10 9 8 7 6 5 4 3 2

harper torchbooks

American Studies: General

HENRY ADAMS Degradation of the Democratic Dogma. ‡ *Introduction by Charles Hirsch-feld.* TB/1450

LOUIS D. BRANDEIS: Other People's Money, *and How the Bankers Use It. Ed. with Intro, by Richard M. Abrams* TB/3081

HENRY STEELE COMMAGER, Ed.: The Struggle for Racial Equality TB/1300

CARL N. DEGLER: Out of Our Past: *The Forces that Shaped Modern America* CN/2

CARL N. DEGLER, Ed.: Pivotal Interpretations of American History
Vol. I TB/1240; Vol. II TB/1241

LAWRENCE H. FUCHS, Ed.: American Ethnic Politics TB/1368

ROBERT L. HEILBRONER: The Limits of American Capitalism TB/1305

JOHN HIGHAM, Ed.: The Reconstruction of American History TB/1068

ROBERT H. JACKSON: The Supreme Court in the American System of Government TB/1106

JOHN F. KENNEDY: A Nation of Immigrants. *Illus. Revised and Enlarged. Introduction by Robert F. Kennedy* TB/1118

RICHARD B. MORRIS: Fair Trial: *Fourteen Who Stood Accused, from Anne Hutchinson to Alger Hiss* TB/1335

GUNNAR MYRDAL: An American Dilemma: *The Negro Problem and Modern Democracy. Introduction by the Author.*
Vol. I TB/1443; Vol. II TB/1444

GILBERT OSOFSKY, Ed.: The Burden of Race: *A Documentary History of Negro-White Relations in America* TB/1405

ARNOLD ROSE: The Negro in America: *The Condensed Version of Gunnar Myrdal's An American Dilemma. Second Edition* TB/3048

JOHN E. SMITH: Themes in American Philosophy: *Purpose, Experience and Community* TB/1466

WILLIAM R. TAYLOR: Cavalier and Yankee: *The Old South and American National Character* TB/1474

American Studies: Colonial

BERNARD BAILYN: The New England Merchants in the Seventeenth Century TB/1149

ROBERT E. BROWN: Middle-Class Democracy and Revolution in Massachusetts, 1691–1780. *New Introduction by Author* TB/1413

JOSEPH CHARLES: The Origins of the American Party System TB/1049

WESLEY FRANK CRAVEN: The Colonies in Transition: 1660-1712† TB/3084

CHARLES GIBSON: Spain in America † TB/3077

CHARLES GIBSON, Ed.: The Spanish Tradition in America + HR/1351

LAWRENCE HENRY GIPSON: The Coming of the Revolution: 1763-1775. † *Illus.* TB/3007

JACK P. GREENE, Ed.: Great Britain and the American Colonies: 1606-1763. + *Introduction by the Author* HR/1477

AUBREY C. LAND, Ed.: Bases of the Plantation Society + HR/1429

PERRY MILLER: Errand Into the Wilderness TB/1139

PERRY MILLER & T. H. JOHNSON, Ed.: The Puritans: *A Sourcebook of Their Writings*
Vol. I TB/1093; Vol. II TB/1094

EDMUND S. MORGAN: The Puritan Family: *Religion and Domestic Relations in Seventeenth Century New England* TB/1227

WALLACE NOTESTEIN: The English People on the Eve of Colonization: 1603-1630. † *Illus.* TB/3006

LOUIS B. WRIGHT: The Cultural Life of the American Colonies: 1607-1763. † *Illus.* TB/3005

YVES F. ZOLTVANY, Ed.: The French Tradition in America + HR/1425

American Studies: The Revolution to 1860

JOHN R. ALDEN: The American Revolution: 1775-1783. † *Illus.* TB/3011

RAY A. BILLINGTON: The Far Western Frontier: 1830-1860. † *Illus.* TB/3012

STUART BRUCHEY: The Roots of American Economic Growth, 1607-1861: *An Essay in Social Causation. New Introduction by the Author.* TB/1350

NOBLE E. CUNNINGHAM, JR., Ed.: The Early Republic, 1789-1828 + HR/1394

GEORGE DANGERFIELD: The Awakening of American Nationalism, 1815-1828. † *Illus.* TB/3061

---

† The New American Nation Series, edited by Henry Steele Commager and Richard B. Morris.
‡ American Perspectives series, edited by Bernard Wishy and William E. Leuchtenburg.
a History of Europe series, edited by J. H. Plumb.
§ The Library of Religion and Culture, edited by Benjamin Nelson.
‖ Researches in the Social, Cultural, and Behavioral Sciences, edited by Benjamin Nelson.
Σ Harper Modern Science Series, edited by James A. Newman.
° Not for sale in Canada.
+ Documentary History of the United States series, edited by Richard B. Morris.
# Documentary History of Western Civilization series, edited by Eugene C. Black and Leonard W. Levy.
Λ The Economic History of the United States series, edited by Henry David et al.
¶ European Perspectives series, edited by Eugene C. Black.
** Contemporary Essays series, edited by Leonard W. Levy.
* The Stratum Series, edited by John Hale.

CLEMENT EATON: The Freedom-of-Thought Struggle in the Old South. *Revised and Enlarged. Illus.* TB/1150
CLEMENT EATON: The Growth of Southern Civilization, 1790-1860. † *Illus.* TB/3040
ROBERT H. FERRELL, Ed.: Foundations of American Diplomacy, 1775-1872 + HR/1393
LOUIS FILLER: The Crusade against Slavery: 1830-1860. † *Illus.* TB/3029
WILLIM W. FREEHLING: Prelude to Civil War: *The Nullification Controversy in South Carolina, 1816-1836* TB/1359
PAUL W. GATES: The Farmer's Age: *Agriculture, 1815-1860* △ TB/1398
THOMAS JEFFERSON: Notes on the State of Virginia. ‡ *Edited by Thomas P. Abernethy* TB/3052
FORREST MCDONALD, Ed.: Confederation and Constitution, 1781-1789 + HR/1396
JOHN C. MILLER: The Federalist Era: 1789-1801. † *Illus.* TB/3027
RICHARD B. MORRIS: The American Revolution Reconsidered TB/1363
CURTIS P. NETTELS: The Emergence of a National Economy, 1775-1815 △ TB/1438
DOUGLASS C. NORTH & ROBERT PAUL THOMAS, Eds.: *The Growth of the American Economy ot 1860* + HR/1352
R. B. NYE: The Cultural Life of the New Nation: 1776-1830. † *Illus.* TB/3026
GILBERT OSOFSKY, Ed.: Puttin' On Ole Massa: *The Slave Narratives of Henry Bibb, William Wells Brown, and Solomon Northup* ‡ TB/1432
JAMES PARTON: The Presidency of Andrew Jackson. *From Volume III of the Life of Andrew Jackson. Ed. with Intro. by Robert V. Remini* TB/3080
FRANCIS S. PHILBRICK: The Rise of the West, 1754-1830. † *Illus.* TB/3067
MARSHALL SMELSER: The Democratic Republic, 1801-1815 + TB/1406
JACK M. SOSIN, Ed.: The Opening of the West + HR/1424
GEORGE ROGERS TAYLOR: The Transportation Revolution, 1815-1860 △ TB/1347
A. F. TYLER: Freedom's Ferment: *Phases of American Social History from the Revolution to the Outbreak of the Civil War. Illus.* TB/1074
GLYNDON G. VAN DEUSEN: The Jacksonian Era: 1828-1848. † *Illus.* TB/3028
LOUIS B. WRIGHT: Culture on the Moving Frontier TB/1053

American Studies: The Civil War to 1900

W. R. BROCK: An American Crisis: *Congress and Reconstruction, 1865-67* ° TB/1283
T. C. COCHRAN & WILLIAM MILLER: The Age of Enterprise: *A Social History of Industrial America* TB/1054
W. A. DUNNING: Reconstruction, Political and Economic: 1865-1877 TB/1073
HAROLD U. FAULKNER: Politics, Reform and Expansion: 1890-1900. † *Illus.* TB/3020
GEORGE M. FREDRICKSON: The Inner Civil War: *Northern Intellectuals and the Crisis of the Union* TB/1358
JOHN A. GARRATY: The New Commonwealth, 1877-1890 + TB/1410
JOHN A. GARRATY, Ed.: The Transformation of American Society, 1870-1890 + HR/1395
HELEN HUNT JACKSON: A Century of Dishonor: *The Early Crusade for Indian Reform.* † *Edited by Andrew F. Rolle* TB/3063

WILLIAM G. MCLOUGHLIN, Ed.: The American Evangelicals, 1800-1900: An Anthology ‡ TB/1382
JAMES S. PIKE: The Prostrate State: *South Carolina under Negro Government.* ‡ *Intro. by Robert F. Durden* TB/3085
FRED A. SHANNON: The Farmer's Last Frontier: *Agriculture, 1860-1897* TB/1348
VERNON LANE WHARTON: The Negro in Mississippi, 1865-1890 TB/1178

American Studies: The Twentieth Century

RICHARD M. ABRAMS, Ed.: The Issues of the Populist and Progressive Eras, 1892-1912 + HR/1428
RAY STANNARD BAKER: Following the Color Line: *American Negro Citizenship in Progressive Era.* ‡ *Edited by Dewey W. Grantham, Jr. Illus.* TB/3053
RANDOLPH S. BOURNE: War and the Intellectuals: *Collected Essays, 1915-1919.* ‡ *Edited by Carl Resek* TB/3043
A. RUSSELL BUCHANAN: The United States and World War II. † *Illus.*
Vol. I TB/3044; Vol. II TB/3045
THOMAS C. COCHRAN: The American Business System: *A Historical Perspective, 1900-1955* TB/1080
FOSTER RHEA DULLES: America's Rise to World Power: 1898-1954. † *Illus.* TB/3021
HAROLD U. FAULKNER: The Decline of Laissez Faire, 1897-1917 TB/1397
JOHN D. HICKS: Republican Ascendancy: 1921-1933. † *Illus.* TB/3041
WILLIAM E. LEUCHTENBURG: Franklin D. Roosevelt and the New Deal: 1932-1940. † *Illus.* TB/3025
WILLIAM E. LEUCHTENBURG, Ed.: The New Deal: *A Documentary History* + HR/1354
ARTHUR S. LINK: Woodrow Wilson and the Progressive Era: 1910-1917. † *Illus.* TB/3023
BROADUS MITCHELL: Depression Decade: *From New Era through New Deal, 1929-1941* + TB/1439
GEORGE E. MOWRY: The Era of Theodore Roosevelt and the Birth of Modern America: 1900-1912. † *Illus.* TB/3022
GEORGE SOULE: Prosperity Decade: *From War to Depression, 1917-1929* △ TB/1349
TWELVE SOUTHERNERS: I'll Take My Stand: *The South and the Agrarian Tradition. Intro. by Louis D. Rubin, Jr.; Biographical Essays by Virginia Rock* TB/1072

Art, Art History, Aesthetics

ERWIN PANOFSKY: Renaissance and Renascences in Western Art. *Illus.* TB/1447
ERWIN PANOFSKY: Studies in Iconology: *Humanistic Themes in the Art of the Renaissance. 180 illus.* TB/1077
OTTO VON SIMSON: The Gothic Cathedral: *Origins of Gothic Architecture and the Medieval Concept of Order. 58 illus.* TB/2018
HEINRICH ZIMMER: Myths and Symbols in Indian Art and Civilization. *70 illus.* TB/2005

Asian Studies

WOLFGANG FRANKE: China and the West: *The Cultural Encounter, 13th to 20th Centuries. Trans. by R. A. Wilson* TB/1326
L. CARRINGTON GOODRICH: A Short History of the Chinese People. *Illus.* TB/3015

5

EDWARD CONZE et al, Editors: Buddhist Texts through the Ages TB/113
H. G. CREEL: Confucius and the Chinese Way TB/63
FRANKLIN EDGERTON, Trans. & Ed.: The Bhagavad Gita TB/115
SWAMI NIKHILANANDA, Trans. & Ed.: The Upanishads TB/114

Religion: Philosophy, Culture, and Society

NICOLAS BERDYAEV: The Destiny of Man TB/61
RUDOLF BULTMANN: History and Eschatology: The Presence of Eternity ° TB/91
LUDWIG FEUERBACH: The Essence of Christianity. § Introduction by Karl Barth. Foreword by H. Richard Niebuhr TB/11
ADOLF HARNACK: What Is Christianity? § Introduction by Rudolf Bultmann TB/17
KYLE HASELDEN: The Racial Problem in Christian Perspective TB/116
IMMANUEL KANT: Religion Within the Limits of Reason Alone. § Introduction by Theodore M. Greene and John Silber TB/67
H. RICHARD NIEBUHR: Christ and Culture TB/3
H. RICHARD NIEBUHR: The Kingdom of God in America TB/49

Science and Mathematics

W. E. LE GROS CLARK: The Antecedents of Man: An Introduction to the Evolution of the Primates. ° Illus. TB/559
ROBERT E. COKER: Streams, Lakes, Ponds. Illus. TB/586
ROBERT E. COKER: This Great and Wide Sea: An Introduction to Oceanography and Marine Biology. Illus. TB/551
F. K. HARE: The Restless Atmosphere TB/560
WILLARD VAN ORMAN QUINE: Mathematical Logic TB/558

Science: Philosophy

J. M. BOCHENSKI: The Methods of Contemporary Thought. Tr. by Peter Caws TB/1377
J. BRONOWSKI: Science and Human Values. Revised and Enlarged. Illus. TB/505
WERNER HEISENBERG: Physics and Philosophy: The Revolution in Modern Science. Introduction by F. S. C. Northrop TB/549
KARL R. POPPER: Conjectures and Refutations: The Growth of Scientific Knowledge TB/1376
KARL R. POPPER: The Logic of Scientific Discovery TB/576

Sociology and Anthropology

REINHARD BENDIX: Work and Authority in Industry: Ideologies of Management in the Course of Industrialization TB/3035
BERNARD BERELSON, Ed., The Behavioral Sciences Today TB/1127
KENNETH B. CLARK: Dark Ghetto: Dilemmas of Social Power. Foreword by Gunnar Myrdal TB/1317

KENNETH CLARK & JEANNETTE HOPKINS: A Relevant War Against Poverty: A Study of Community Action Programs and Observable Social Change TB/1480
LEWIS COSER, Ed.: Political Sociology TB/1293
ALLISON DAVIS & JOHN DOLLARD: Children of Bondage: The Personality Development of Negro Youth in the Urban South || TB/3049
ST. CLAIR DRAKE & HORACE R. CAYTON: Black Metropolis: A Study of Negro Life in a Northern City. Introduction by Everett C. Hughes. Tables, maps, charts, and graphs Vol. I TB/1086; Vol. II TB/1087
PETER F. DRUCKER: The New Society: The Anatomy of Industrial Order TB/1082
CHARLES Y. GLOCK & RODNEY STARK: Christian Beliefs and Anti-Semitism. Introduction by the Authors TB/1454
ALVIN W. GOULDNER: The Hellenic World TB/1479
R. M. MACIVER: Social Causation TB/1153
GARY T. MARX: Protest and Prejudice: A Study of Belief in the Black Community TB/1435
ROBERT K. MERTON, LEONARD BROOM, LEONARD S. COTTRELL, JR., Editors: Sociology Today: Problems and Prospects ||
Vol. I TB/1173; Vol. II TB/1174
GILBERT OSOFSKY, Ed.: The Burden of Race: A Documentary History of Negro-White Relations in America TB/1405
GILBERT OSOFSKY: Harlem: The Making of a Ghetto: Negro New York 1890-1930 TB/1381
TALCOTT PARSONS & EDWARD A. SHILS, Editors: Toward a General Theory of Action: Theoretical Foundations for the Social Sciences TB/1083
PHILIP RIEFF: The Triumph of the Therapeutic: Uses of Faith After Freud TB/1360
JOHN H. ROHRER & MUNRO S. EDMONSON, Eds.: The Eighth Generation Grows Up: Cultures and Personalities of New Orleans Negroes || TB/3050
ARNOLD ROSE: The Negro in America: The Condensed Version of Gunnar Myrdal's An American Dilemma. Second Edition TB/3048
GEORGE ROSEN: Madness in Society: Chapters in the Historical Sociology of Mental Illness. || Preface by Benjamin Nelson TB/1337
PHILIP SELZNICK: TVA and the Grass Roots: A Study in the Sociology of Formal Organization TB/1230
PITIRIM A. SOROKIN: Contemporary Sociological Theories: Through the First Quarter of the Twentieth Century TB/3046
MAURICE R. STEIN: The Eclipse of Community: An Interpretation of American Studies TB/1128
FERDINAND TONNIES: Community and Society: Gemeinschaft und Gesellschaft. Translated and Edited by Charles P. Loomis TB/1116
W. LLOYD WARNER and Associates: Democracy in Jonesville: A Study in Quality and Inequality || TB/1129
W. LLOYD WARNER: Social Class in America: The Evaluation of Status TB/1013
FLORIAN ZNANIECKI: The Social Role of the Man of Knowledge. Introduction by Lewis A. Coser TB/1372